The
Secrets of the Threshold

SERIES XXIX

A Course of Eight Lectures
BY RUDOLF STEINER, Ph.D.
(Munich, 24th to 31st August, 1913).

(Shorthand Report unrevised by the Lecturer)

LONDON :
ANTHROPOSOPHICAL PUBLISHING Co.

NEW YORK :
ANTHROPOSOPHIC PRESS

The
Secrets of the Threshold

RUDOLF STEINER Ph.D.

Authorized Translation
Edited by H. Collison

Printed in Guernsey C.I., British Isles, by the Star and Gazette Co. Ltd.

SYNOPSIS OF CONTENTS

This Synopsis is only intended for the possible convenience of Students, and has no claim to be authoritative.

LECTURE 1. This lecture contains the first reference to Eurhythmy and deals entirely with the fourth Mystery Play '*The Soul's Awakening*'. Schuré's drama—'*The Guardian of the Soul*'. Charlemagne and the Filioque. Remarks on life after death as shown in the last Mystery Play. Most souls sleep through the cosmic midnight or Saturn time; those who are prepared keep awake. Recollection during earth life only occurs when steadiness or calmness of soul has been acquired. The sense of words differs according to context and by whom spoken. The soul awakens in different ways; but perfect calm is absolutely necessary. ' Hide sense obscure within clear words.'

LECTURE 2. Ahriman and Lucifer are both necessary, they cannot be driven away, but they must be balanced. Their actions in their own sphere are justified, but not outside it. Ahriman rightly lord of death and the mineral world. The mineral world exists in all realms of external nature and in ourselves. Ahriman oversteps his bounds when he enters the thinking of man. His duty is to regulate the brain towards decay, but he wrongfully strives to snatch it from decay and makes man want to separate thought from cosmic order. Hence materialism and materialistic thought. He is always watching for man to think of the spirit world and then sends shadows and phantoms of physical human thought snatched from its mother soil. If by false theory we try to drive him away we fall into the impulses of Lucifer. False asceticism. Ahriman is spiritual and in external nature. Lucifer is psychic and his impulses are within. Lucifer's duty is to prevent man from being absorbed in the physical world. Art, Philosophy. Lucifer is properly lord of desire, but wrong when he tries to detach it from cosmic order. Love for sake of another is absolutely protected from Lucifer. The cause of love must lie in the person loved not in the person who loves. It applies to beings of other kingdoms, animals, etc. Where a person loves because he has in him certain propensities which are thereby pleased, this is egoistic. It must exist when applied to the spirit world in our desires to be more spiritual. But Lucifer wrongly mixes up the two worlds and tries to draw man into an exclusive Luciferic kingdom (*e.g.*, medical advice to men) [See reference to Theosophical Society]. Cranks, false idealism is the shadow side of Lucifer. Nature allows no 'ostrich policy.' Every soul desires the spirit world, but many souls force themselves to be unconscious of the desire. And because what is repressed on one side will appear on another, this desire is transformed to sensual impulses, which become perverse. The threshold between the physical world and the spirit world must be carefully observed and not confused as Lucifer would wish. The danger of crossing the Threshold improperly. 'Nibbling dainties' in the spirit world. Pictures become densified and confusion arises between real and fanciful. Schopenhauer and Kant refuted by living facts. False pictures the booty of Ahriman. When a soul nibbles at spirit world and gets something, care must be had on return to physical plane not to use mode of thought suitable to spiritual, or Ahriman will seize it. We must not carry into spirit world desires of physical plane or Lucifer will seize us. Vanity and ambition are so deeply rooted in human nature that it is difficult to admit the possession of it. These are the worst emotions. Necessity for calm at the soul's awakening.

LECTURE 3.   Element-world, the first condition is the ability to transform into a foreign being. Etheric body an entity of element-world and capable of metamorphosis. On the physical plane, the etheric body must conform to physical plane, *i.e.*, distinct personality. The methods of one plane must not be taken to another. Sleeping and waking on physical plane, volition and transformation on element-plane. For transformation, imagination or thinking is required; for volition, the feeling of self must be strengthened. In physical world, the physical body helps to consciousness of Ego. In element-world, will is required. In element-world both states may exist together. Thinking differs in the two worlds: in the physical world, thoughts are passive; in element-world thoughts are living entities, 'like an ant-heap.' In element-world we see an entity by sympathy or antipathy. But we must receive it with equanimity. In element-world the self is maintained without external force, it is volitional. Strong volition is succeeded by isolation.

The will must be developed on physical plane, so too the moral standard. Clairvoyance—lotus flowers. Moral firmness the element-backbone. In element-world Lucifer and Ahriman different from physical world. In the element-world Lucifer from outside tries to seize the lotus flowers, and Ahriman tries to settle in the element-backbone. There an alliance is formed over our ambition, vanity, etc., and we become imprisoned.

LECTURE 4.   In ascent from element-world to spirit-world, everything of the sense world must be abandoned. The scenery of spirit-land in the fourth Play is exactly as seen in the spirit world. These pictures one reads like Cosmic writing. To do this one must be calm and receptive. Unnecessary to try to be clairvoyant. One cannot prove spirit by processes of physical. Nonsense and vanity about reincarnation. Test of a previous incarnation is that its knowledge must be independent of anything with which we are at present connected or that can be applied to present life. In spirit-world thoughts are beings and beings thoughts more real than men of flesh and blood. Words move and when spoken a thing takes place. The Cosmic Word.

LECTURE 5.   ' Professor Capesius.' Frequently historians of this epoch have been connected with mysteries of Ancient Egypt. Balde and wife. Very important description of Lucifer, Ahriman. Haeckelism, atoms. The importance of the law of number and measure. Seek and find the triad in everything. Pythagoras. The legend of the castle. Solitary thought is Lucifer. This is made permanent by Ahriman in writing. The Word comes between. Libraries are the citadels of Ahriman. Lucifer has divided and separated the Word so as to isolate the words for his special island. Tower of Babel. The Word of the Spirit must be the balance. Mere thinking is Lucifer, mere listening is Ahriman. Meditation, so that one sees and hears one's own thoughts, comes between.

LECTURE 6.   Roman letter Ahriman. Gothic Lucifer : should be balanced by mutual national respect and understanding. Modern superficiality in regard to spirit. Without being too rigid note the following : Architecture and Sculpture exposed to Ahriman (the real rulers are Spirits of Form, so Ahriman is perfectly legitimate); Music and Poetry to Lucifer ; Poetry very national. Painting is a combination between Sculpture and Architecture on the one hand, and Music and Poetry on the other. In the physical world one discovers one's physical body, in the element-world one's etheric body, in the Spirit-world one's real self in one's astral body as a second Being. This other self goes from incarnation to incarnation. We cannot see it in the physical world because it is in the Spirit-world. But it is intricately bound up with man, works in 'Inspiration' upon karma. But all that takes place in Spirit-world stamps itself on the physical world. Inspirations are used by the Cosmic Word as the Inspirers of human fate. When one has met one's other self one no longer considers one's personality within the accustomed limits, but one expands. One can bring nothing from one world into the other ; except the memory of what one thought, willed and felt in the physical world. One experiences then that one is only a memory. One learns Lucifer is a 'has been.' He fights to get present and future into the lap of the past. Then one's memory converses with living thought beings in the environment. Then one becomes a spirit being, filled with fresh spirit-matter and a triad is again formed.

LECTURE 7. No royal road, each soul has its own path. In Spirit-world, Feeling, Thinking, Willing become objective as Philia, Astrid, Luna. The 'double' explained. Ahriman tries to give everything the form of the physical plane. There are parts of our soul over which we have not yet complete control ; it becomes independent etheric and Ahriman gives it human form in the element-world and it is called our 'double.' The Spirits of Form also rule in the physical world. Ahriman fills a portion of the soul with self-seeking elements and this is part of the etheric body. Johannes in First Play only gets 'Imaginative' experiences with all their mistakes, subjective. In the Temple scene he sees things far in advance of his condition. In the Second Play, his experience objective. In the Third Play he reaches the spiritual subjective world where Ahriman meets him subjectively and Lucifer objectively. Johannes oscillates greatly between the two selves. The 'Youth of Johannes' is his unredeemed karma. To this Lucifer has access, for he can take a portion of the etheric body and ensoul it with unredeemed karma. It ought to be within Johannes and not outside him. The 'Other Philia' shows Johannes that he has created an illegitimate soul-child. Maria's development is almost normal. Philia in scene 9 is absent ; this is to show that in Maria the spirit soul and rational soul are developed in her more regularly than the sentient soul. Johannes' development is not normal and his Higher Self illumines his inner conditions so that they show in various forms. The Other Philia is, in a sense, the Other Self within the depths of the soul ; connected with Supreme Love leading to Higher worlds. In Spirit-world everything is in transformation and so Johannes is confused. He, at first, mistakes the Double for Philia. He has a triad of experiences : twice ' Other Philia ' once only the ' Double.' Lucifer makes part of our unredeemed karma into independent phantom beings of the Spirit-world. Johannes is gradually cured of his subjective leanings by the words ' Magical weaving of thine own being.' Even in Spirit-world it is long before one finds one's true ego of which the ego in the physical world is only a phantom. This is attempted by Strader in Scene 3, the last play, where he tries to obliterate everything concerning his past, and to forget himself. Unconsciously this happens every night.

LECTURE 8.   Lucifer and Ahriman change their rôle in different epochs. Now they have formed an alliance and made a tangled web around us, as we see in many social agitations. On leaving the element-world man leaves his etheric body and lives in his astral body in the Spirit-world ; then he leaves his astral body and is in his true ego in the super Spirit-world. The true ego is always, however, our companion. When we meet him at the Threshold he is in a peculiar garb, in all our weaknesses that attach us to the physical world. This is the Guardian of the Threshold, but he is more foreign to us than any person in the earth-world and different from any spirit-beings in the Spirit-world. We stand before him every night, but the soul in terror deadens its consciousness and we mercifully see nothing. This is the best moment for Ahriman. Ahriman and Lucifer here make an alliance but the Guardian shuts the door. Nothing wrong can then happen, but if there is a craving to enter in order to pilfer the Spirit-world, the pilferings are densified by Ahriman and the soul gets hallucinations. We must strengthen will and feeling of self before entering. Before passing the Guardian real genuine and unsparing self-knowledge is necessary. This is harder than people admit. [References to Mrs. Besant's book.] An excellent exercise when we consider ourselves aggrieved : admit the possibility that we rather than the others are in error. We must cultivate a feeling of self for the Spirit-world but must abandon it upon re-entering the physical world. Maria truly says that on the physical plane men are asleep but in the spirit plane awake. The feeling of self on the physical plane is brought about by love for others rather than for oneself. This is protected from Lucifer and Ahriman by special means. Often the man who admits he is selfish is less so than those who deal in theosophical abstractions about love and tolerance. The want of sympathy thus exhibited is the creation of terrible forms in the Spirit-world. In the Soul-world after death man's gaze is chiefly fixed on the fate of his etheric body and its transformations in the element-world form the environment of the soul in kamaloca. Comparison between good-natured and ill-natured fellow. After this comes the life in the astral body which begins to loosen and expand and separate from the man. With this astral body we lose ' our past.' Self-less un-egoistic souls—called weak in life—are the souls strong after death ; they can see for a long time the memory of the physical. Memory disappears and returns in a changed manner. Before this return, about half way between death and new life, one experiences oneself in the true ego, and then comes what is right for the next life. This moment is the cosmic midnight. Third scene, last Play ; Strader's approaching death. The necessity for a feeling of responsibility in our movement.

THE SECRETS OF THE THRESHOLD

DR. RUDOLF STEINER

LECTURE I

Munich, 24th August, 1913.

You have had to witness how we have been forced to begin our Festival on this occasion with an omission. To my great regret we could not in this Festival give what had been intended, namely, a performance of ' La Sœur Gardienne ' *The Guardian of the Soul*, by our revered friend, Edouard Schuré. Owing to the most manifold reasons, we have had to defer its presentation on the stage. In one way this was the more grievous because, just in our days, just at the present time, it would have seemed important to place before our minds the meaning and significance of this work of our respected Edouard Schuré. In it outward expression is given to certain beating waves and currents in the evolution of humanity which might make many a thing comprehensible in the frequently agitating experiences of the present. These experiences pass across our souls without the possibility of indicating with the brain of Western Europeans—in other words, with an understanding that has to be developed on the physical plane—the deeper foundations of these experiences.

For a more deeply thinking mind, it is positively striking to see how what is of the greatest significance is convulsing, as it were, the souls of the peoples on the east of Europe ; how many a thing is happening there which only admits

1

of explanation when we take into consideration the wave-beats that, under the surface of the physical world, are pulsing in the lives of the peoples. It is in certain degree remarkable how little the intellectual thought of Western Europe thinks of bringing the deeper foundations of these agitating experiences to the understanding of heart and soul. And, through the direct impressions of the present time, one might say that it would seem to be a karmic command to see a drama played before the soul's eye which brings to the surface the contrasts in the souls of the peoples.

It would have had a special attraction for us—not only aesthetically, but also with regard to the understanding of much that is taking place in our times—if we could have had before our soul's eye the contrast that would have been made apparent in *The Soul's Guardian* by Edouard Schuré,—the contrast between what has remained in Western Europe as an impulse, as a colouring from the old Celtic Folk-Soul, and which meets us in one part of the dramatis personae of this play, and the really Franco-Roman element in the rest ; and if we could, moreover, have perceived how the waves, formed in the occult world, are playing their part in human life, expressing themselves outwardly in the life of the senses. For in this drama there comes to expression how, through certain happenings, an untruth is, as it were, spreading itself abroad in the physical world ; so that the relations which exist between the characters give expression to this untruth ; and how from the substrata of the life of the soul—in this case from that which plays a part in the secrets of the blood—the truth is then, to a certain extent, poured into the untrue conditions of the world of the senses. In this drama we should have seen all this expressed before our soul's eye. It is indeed important in our day to let such things work upon our souls, now, at this time, when, before our very eyes, in Europe itself, events are taking place into which there really penetrate the forces of national temperaments, dominant beneath the surface, and which cannot be understood unless we fix our mental gaze upon these national temperaments. What is playing its part in external life, rising up karmically to the surface, is that which laid hold of the national temperaments many centuries ago in the East and South-east of Europe. It might be said that karmic things are now taking place imperceptibly to the external world, connected with what only symptomatically finds expression on the physical plane, really finding expression on the physical plane in four syllables. What is now attaining to karmic expression was prepared when there entered into the souls of the European peoples, dividing and cleaving them into East and West, the celebrated and much disputed ‘Filioque.’ Nowadays, what does our present mentality, with its understanding, care about that which formerly led to the division between Eastern and Western Europe, as to whether what is designated as the Holy Ghost proceeds only from the Father, according to the declaration of the East, or from the Son also, as declared by the West ?   There were good reasons why the west, at that time, added the ' Filioque ' to the procession of the Holy Ghost from the Father, for all the forces which developed in the West of Europe and which gave the impulses for European civilisation, are connected with this.   We are not here concerned with all the theological strife which grew out of this Credo of the various confessions of faith, but to us it is important that psychic events once found expression in such a way that the former single confession of faith was so divided that there were those who said that the Holy Ghost proceeds from the Father and the Son, whereas others believed that the Holy Ghost proceeds from the Father only.

That expresses what is working into our own times, living and pulsing in the subterranean depths, and which can only be understood when one enters a little into the mysterious activity of the occult substrata in the souls of the nations. It was at the time when the sword of Charlemagne enforced, on behalf of the West against the East, the confession of faith that the Holy Spirit proceeds from the Father and the Son,—for it was not the Papal Church but the sword of Charlemagne that enforced this,—it was then that the foundation was laid in the civilisation of Europe for that which we now again see pulsing upwards in powerful and convulsing wave-beats.   Thus the meditating upon this drama which is founded upon these National Souls, might have thrown many a ray of light into the experiences of the present.

What finally decided us to put off this performance was a fact which on the one hand gives us great pleasure, namely, that so many had announced their desire to be present at the performance of *The Guardian of the Threshold*, and *The Soul's Awakening* (which is now the title of our last play), that many of our friends would have had to be refused if we had wanted to carry through our original programme.   Perhaps but for this circumstance it would still have been possible to carry out our original programme.   All was so far ready : even the decorations were thoroughly completed and all the costumes made.   And if, as we have said, the above circumstance had not arisen, we might have thought of producing this third piece also, only we should have had to turn away a number of our friends from participation in the festival performances. Naturally it is more permissible to put off one of the dramas than to exclude from the actual performances friends who wish to be present.

What we should have gained by the performance of this drama is also connected with the fact that in it we have a work of one whom we respect so highly—Edouard Schuré.   When we mention his name we must remember

3

that we have, in the man who bears it, one who through his work, ' Les Grands Initiés,' *The Great Initiates*, and through his other works, is, in a certain sense, the first standard-bearer of the esoteric movement in the West, to which we desire to devote all our powers. Again and again we ought to reflect upon what has come about through the epoch-making works of Edouard Schuré, for the present and the future evolution of mankind. Hence, not only do I myself wish from the depths of my heart, but also from those of all our friends assembled here, to greet Edouard Schuré with the greatest pleasure, and to have him with us during our festival and cycle once more at Munich. He is present at the morning lectures ; but there are occasions when we shall be all together, when all our friends will have the opportunity of personally being near the man who, with lofty genius and with a deep insight into esoteric relations, again out of his innermost impulse placed himself at our side at the present juncture, when we are involved, as you all know, in a struggle which was thrust upon us, which certainly was not of our own seeking.*

We have had further proof of the inner bond with Edouard Shuré in the open letter which has been repeatedly printed and also in our *Mitteilungen* which you will find bound together with the excellent brochure by our respected friend, Eugène Levy. As I say, Schuré has, with this letter, ranged himself on our side, a letter that has thrown important rays of light as to where Truth and enmity against the Truth—for such it must be called—is to be found, in regard to our endeavours.

It is deeply characteristic, my dear friends, that although from the other side and only after some time—so that, as one might say, it is easy to note the inner opposition, and that they would willingly see a veil drawn over the admission—they have decided to withdraw the senseless reproach of my being a Jesuit ; yet they could not refrain from again giving with this withdrawal what may be called an insult towards what Edouard Schuré, from an earnest sense of truth, brought out in his public letter. The difficulties, in themselves no light ones, that have met us in the presentation of the Munich performances, have been increased by the fact that there was thrust upon us here this strife (which we need not open up again), a strife that has cost us so much labour and thought, and one which was, in truth, quite unnecessary, the continuance of which will also be quite unnecessary.

In the interests of Truth we must now, for the sake of our friends, make a passing allusion to what has happened. In addition to works of which I have already spoken, I will now mention the excellent book by our friend, Levy, now

* Reference is made to Mrs. Besant, and her Theosophical Society.

to be had also in German, the brochure by Dr. Unger, those of Frau Wolfram and Herr Walther—writings which have really been wrung from our friends, for, as a matter of fact, each of them had something better to do than to mix themselves in a struggle that was so unnecessary and so much against the Truth. It will be needful for our friends that these books should not be merely written but also read ; for the time will come when those of our friends who take the Truth earnestly will have to know all this, unedifying as such knowledge may be. It is just from this side that our work at Munich has encountered many a sore hindrance of late.

When I speak of this work as I should like also to do this year, it must be mentioned that for those persons who have had to carry out a difficult and wearing work behind the scenes on behalf of our Munich performances this labour was made no lighter by the fact that one drama has had to fall through. As a consequence of that, the whole arrangement had to be altered, and thus the work was not lessened, but rather increased in difficulty and amount. It must not be thought that where the chief burden fell anything was lightened by the omission of one of the dramas, for this work, which lay principally in the hands of Frl. Stinde and Frau Gräfin Kalckreuth and their helpers, was considerably increased. This year also there is a need, which I feel with my whole heart, to point out the devoted and self-sacrificing manner in which a great number of our friends have again given themselves to the carrying out of our Munich undertaking. The latter can only be brought about by the fact that a great many of our friends make this willing self-offering. The preparations had to begin already in June. Our artists, Herr Linde, Herr Haas and Herr Volckert, had already been obliged to devote themselves to a long task, and, as has been said, it had been handed in completely finished. And with them a whole troop of persons silently devoted themselves to the work behind the scenes, or even before the scenes could come into being.

It is really beautiful, and it will always be so again and again, to see this self-sacrifice. Only to mention one thing as symptomatic of the rest ; one of our friends to whom two great rôles had been assigned, one of which goes through *The Guardian of the Threshold* and *The Soul's Awakening*, and the other would have been in the piece by Schuré—this friend did not even know if he would be able to stand the many rehearsals which would have had to be held for the three pieces, and yet he zealously undertook the task. All these are things showing how greatly devotion and readiness to make sacrifices have gradually grown in an extended circle within our Anthroposophical Society. The friends who—as has been said—had to begin very early with their labours, the above-mentioned artists, also Fräulein von Eckhardstein, who directs the making of the costumes, had to devote themselves entirely to the work from the beginning of June. Those who have to take part in the performances are busy the whole day, so that they can hardly undertake anything else during the day. They are already known to our friends in the Anthroposophical Society, and the friends who have devoted themselves to this work will excuse me from mentioning them individually by name, for were I to do so I should have to go through a long, long list. They will not take it amiss on my part if this year again I only give general expression to the gratitude with which my heart overflows towards all those who have contributed their labours, and certainly also the gratitude felt by all who in any way whatsoever have been enabled to enjoy what has been prepared by our friends for these Munich performances.

Even if, to a certain degree, opponents spring up on all sides, yet we also see how our work is spreading ; and already a great number of our friends have shown an interest in what we might call a new branch of our endeavours : expressive gestures, expressive movements carried out in the loftiest spirit, and which has always been called the art of dancing. A number of our friends have had opportunity, and will have still more, of making themselves acquainted with that which here appears as Eurhythmy. At one of our social gatherings we shall have the opportunity of bringing before our friends something of this branch of our activity. This, my dear friends, is in substance what I had to say about our personal matters in introducing our present cycle of lectures.

.   .   .   .

If you remember what you have seen on the stage during the last few days, you will find that it links up in many ways with what we shall be considering in this cycle of lectures. I may say that, owing to various requests, each year I have not only penned an addition, but have also worked out, to a certain extent, what might have been an explanation, a kind of commentary, on our mystery-dramas ; but I have each time laid the thing aside again for the same reason which I have slightly indicated in the preliminary remarks on *The Soul's Awakening*. I do not care to make an intellectual commentary on something that truly had not a theoretical, an intellectual origin, but stands complete in its pictures like an inspiration from the spiritual world, and about which I could say nothing intellectually different from what anyone else could say if he goes into the matter. A certain need exists when such things are given, of letting them speak for themselves, and not sucking them dry, so to speak, in a threadbare, intellectual manner, which can only be thought out by the understanding and by theorising.

And yet, perhaps, we might deal with several points in this course of

6

lectures ; and here I would first of all draw your attention to what was presented to you in the ninth, tenth and thirteenth scenes of *The Soul's Awakening*. In these scenes we have something before us that one might call simple pictorial impressions, whereas, perhaps, many a person might expect that after what has been happening on the stage, in what relates to the Realm of Spirit and the Egyptian initiation, something would be presented that would be more tumultuous, more tragic, something louder—one might say—and not taking place in the stillness of the soul. In that case all would have to be different in the ninth, tenth and thirteenth scenes, and these then would have to appear untrue to occult eyes.

We have before us the development of several souls. On this matter it must at once be said that in the more theoretical descriptions which we have also given for soul-development into the higher worlds, facts are given for indeed every soul concerning the path into the higher worlds ; but that also the soul-development must be different for every soul according to its special kind, character, temperament, and other natural circumstances. Hence we can also gain a deeper understanding of the inward development of the soul when we observe it in its variety,—how it is different for Maria, different for Johannes Thomasius, and again different for the other personages of our drama.

The ninth scene is in the first place dedicated to that psychic moment in Maria wherein there enters into her soul a consciousness of what this soul had experienced in its depths, though not in full consciousness, in the preceding devachanic period, and what it had gone through in a far-off past, at the time when the Egyptian initiation took place. In this time as represented to be taking place in the Spirit-land, we have to do with the experiences of the soul between that death which had taken place after an incarnation in the Middle Ages, and its birth into the present time. The experiences of the *Portal of Initiation, The Soul's Probation, The Soul's Awakening*, and *The Guardian of the Threshold* : all these—with the exception of the episode in *The Soul's Probation*, which represents the spiritual review of his previous life by Capesius, —take place at the present time ; that present time which is linked to the spiritual past which had been spent in devachan between the death of the aforementioned persons after their incarnation in the Middle Ages (this being the contents of the episode in question), and the present life.

The experiences of the souls in their devachanic period differs, according as the souls have gone through this or that preparation on earth. It must be understood to be a significant psychic experience if the soul in the devachanic time goes consciously through what is called the Cosmic Midnight. To souls not prepared for it, this Cosmic Midnight is so experienced that they sleep, as it were, through that time which one may call the Saturn-time in Devachan. For one can designate the successive periods which the souls go through between death and a new birth with reference to the several planets, as the Sun, Mars, Mercury periods, and so on. Many souls sleep, so to say, through this Cosmic Midnight. Prepared souls are awake during the time of their spiritual life in that Cosmic Midnight. It does not as yet follow that souls which, owing to their particular preparation, experience this Cosmic Midnight between death and a new birth in a waking state—it does not follow that these necessarily bring a consciousness of this experience into their earth-life when they come into physical existence. Maria and Johannes Thomasius, having been suitably prepared, experience the Cosmic Midnight in their spiritual time between death and a new birth, yet a kind of dullness of soul spreads over them at the beginning of their earth-life and continues through a long portion of it,—it extended over this experience in the Cosmic Midnight, which then reappeared at a later stage of their present earth-life. It only reappears after a certain calmness and steadiness of soul has been acquired. Significant and profound are the experiences which happen to the soul when it passes through the Cosmic Midnight awake. The earthly memory of this Cosmic Midnight must be a calm inner experience, a luminous inner experience ; for the effect of this experience of the Cosmic Midnight is, that what formerly was only subjective and only worked as a soul-force in the inner being, now appears as living beings before the soul. Thus, as shown in the ninth scene of *The Soul's Awakening*, it presents itself before Maria in the forms of Astrid and Luna, and these appear as living beings ; to Johannes Thomasius the ' other Philia ' becomes a living being of the spiritual world ; and to Capesius, Philia, as she is shown in scene thirteen, is a living being of the spiritual world. These souls had so to feel, so to experience themselves, that what formerly was only an abstract force within them now comes before them in a spiritually tangible form. And that which in a spiritually tangible form thus places itself before the soul as true self-knowledge, must come about in complete soul-calm, as a calm result of meditation ; that is essential if such events are to be experienced in the real, true sense of the word for the real strengthening of the soul. If a person wanted to experience the retrospective memory of the Cosmic Midnight, or such an experience as is represented in the scene of the Egyptian initiation, not in luminous meditation, but in tumultuous tragedy, then he would not be able to experience it at all. Then the spiritual experience that is taking place in the soul would place itself as a dark veil before that soul, so that the impressions would withdraw from the soul's observation. A soul which has experienced the Cosmic Midnight and which has gone with a deep impression through something of the kind shown in

8

the seventh and eighth scenes of *The Soul's Awakening*, can only remember what it has gone through when the soul, in a state of complete and enlightened repose, experiences the harking back of the thoughts to what had been experienced previously, either in the spiritual or in the former earthly incarnation, as is expressed in the words at the beginning of the ninth scene : ' A Soul-star on the border-land of Spirit ! It draws near ; approaches me in spirit-light. With mine own self it comes. As it approaches, its light gains in strength and also in repose. Thou Star within the circle of my spirit, what does thine approach ray forth for my soul's vision ? '

Only when the soul is in this calm mood, so that the experience does not roll upon it with tumultuous tragedy, can one feel as occultly true the arising of the memory of the Cosmic Midnight and the experiences of the previous incarnation. There, where it is experienced, where Cosmic Midnight is gone through, one certainly does experience things of the most profound significance for one's psychic life. There, one experiences what one cannot express otherwise than as follows : In that Cosmic Midnight one experiences things that lie deeply hidden under the surface not only of the sense-world, but also under the surface of many a world into which a dawning clairvoyance leads. The sense-world withdraws ; but also from many a clairvoyant vision which pierces certain strata behind the sense-world, there recedes what we might call—we shall speak of it more at length later on—the Necessities in the cosmic happenings ; those Necessities which are rooted in the foundations of things, within which the deepest part of the human soul is also rooted, but which withdraw from the sight of sense, as well as from a preliminary clairvoyance, and only reveal themselves to the latter when something is experienced such as is pictorially represented in the Saturn Period. For one may say that to such a clairvoyant vision, which must indeed first appear between death and a new birth, it is as if lightning darts across the soul's whole field of vision, which in terrifying brilliancy lights up the Cosmic Necessities, but which is at the same time so blinding that the flashes of cognition die away because of the bright light, and from these dying flashes of cognition there come forth picture-forms, which then enweave themselves into the cosmic warp and woof, like the forms out of which grow the fates of the cosmic beings. One only fathoms the reasons of the fates of the cosmic beings in the foundations of the Necessities when one gazes with glances of cognition, which in cognising expire, killed by the lightning flashes, and transform themselves into shapes that have died but which then live on as the impulse of destiny in life. All that a true self-knowledge finds in itself,—not that self-knowledge about which there is so much gossip in the field of Theosophy, but that most deeply serious self-knowledge which comes in the course of the occult

9

life,—all that the soul perceives within herself with all the imperfections she ascribes to herself, all this is heard at the Cosmic Midnight as if enwoven in rolling cosmic thunder, rumbling in the underground of existence.

All these experiences may pass with great tragedy and with a holy seriousness between death and a new birth as an awakening with respect to the Cosmic Midnight. If the soul is to be ripe enough to allow a consciousness of this to enter into the physical sense world, this must then occur in that quiet clarity of the meditating mood which is hinted at in the words of Maria at the beginning of the ninth scene, fourth play. But then for this soul there must have been repeated within it that which had been experienced within its spiritual life ; as if something of itself, something that belonged intimately to itself,—only that it had not always dwelt in that which one thus calls Self—had approached it from the field of space. That mood in which something like a part of her own self in the spirit world approaches, but as though coming from distant parts of space, we have endeavoured to render in the words spoken by Maria in the Spirit-sphere : (*The Soul's Awakening, page 231.**)

> The flames draw nigh,—they draw nigh with my thought—
> There from my distant cosmic shore of souls ;
> A fierce strife doth draw nigh ;—'tis mine own thought
> Which battles with the thoughts of Lucifer ;—
> Mine own thought battles in another's soul,—
> The hot light issues—out of gloomy cold—
> Like lightning flashes. Is this not soul-light—
> This soul-light—in the cosmic fields of ice ?

The memory of that which is felt and permits of being expressed in such words, can be rendered again in the above-mentioned words of Maria at the beginning of the ninth scene. But what the soul must feel in order to have such a memory of the Cosmic Midnight must also lie in the earth life, so that the human soul indeed goes through events which will bring to its experience feelings of inner tragedy, inner seriousness, inner terror, which it is only possible to express in such words as those put into the mouth of Maria at the end of the fourth scene. There one must have felt that the individual self tears itself away from what one generally calls the inner life ; that the thinking power with which one so trustfully feels oneself connected in life, tears itself out of one's inner being and goes as if into far, far reaches of the field of vision ; and

---

* *Four Mystery Plays*, by Rudolf Steiner. Anthroposophical Publishing Company. In 2 Vols. Price 12s. net.

one must have found in oneself as a living psychic present, that which is expressed in such words as must naturally seem complete nonsense overflowing with contradictions to the external comprehension and the understanding connected with the physical brain. One must first have experienced the feeling of the exit of one's own self, of one's own thought from the inner being, if one wants to experience in complete calm the memory of the Cosmic Midnight. The memory during earth-life must be preceded by the experience of the Cosmic Midnight in the spiritual life, if something similar to what is in the ninth scene is to take place. But in order that that may be possible, again there must already have been the psychic mood expressed at the end of the fourth scene. The flames do in truth depart; they do not come earlier into the earthly-consciousness; they do not approach the repose in meditation until they have first fled away, until this psychic mood has become a truth :—(*The Soul's Awakening, page* 214.)

' The flames fly off,—they fly off with my thought.

And there on distant cosmic shore of souls
A furious fight—my power of thought doth fight—
In stormy chaos—and cold spirit-light—
My thought-power reels ;—the cold light hammers out
Hot waves of darkness from my failing thought.
What now emergeth from the darkling heat ?
Clad in red flames my self storms—to the light ;
To the cold light—of cosmic fields of ice.'

Thus are these things connected, and when they are so connected they then strengthen the inner soul-faculties, so that what was at first only abstract soul-force now appears in ghostly bodily form before the soul,—so that it is at the same time a special entity and we perceive it when Astrid and Luna appear before Maria. These beings, who are real beings and are at the same time experienced as soul-forces, make their appearance so that they can be seen, in company with the Guardian of the Threshold and with Benedictus, as is shown in the ninth scene. But the essential thing is that one perceives the feeling or mood of this Scene when in quite another and more individual manner (so that the soul-force which corresponds to the other Philia becomes endowed with bodily form), the awakening, the remembrance of the Cosmic Midnight and of the preceding Egyptian Age, takes place for Johannes Thomasius. For to a soul so attuned as that of Johannes Thomasius, the saying of the ' other Philia,'

11

'the magic weaving of one's own being,' has its own significance, as has all that is connected with it in the course of the Mystery Drama, and because this is so, the Spirit of Johannes' youth, Benedictus, and Lucifer, appear in the manner in which they are represented towards the end of the tenth scene.

It is necessary that just for this particular scene we should keep in mind that Lucifer here approaches Johannes Thomasius, and that the same words are spoken as at the end of the third scene of *The Guardian of the Threshold*, and how in these words is shown that through all the worlds and through every human life, there goes the conflict of Lucifer, but the feeling which meets the words of Lucifer with those of Benedictus runs through them too. Try to feel what lies in these words which are heard from Lucifer, both at the end of the third scene of *The Guardian of the Threshold*, and at the end of the tenth scene of *The Soul's Awakening*, 'I mean to fight' and the reply thereto. 'And fighting serve the Gods.' (page 266.) At the same time let us carefully note something else ; let us note that the same words are spoken in these two places, but that they can be spoken in such a way that at each time, in these two places, they signify something quite different. The other thing that they signify, at the end of the tenth scene of *The Soul's Awakening*, is determined by the fact that the previous words of Maria had been words altered from others that had been spoken in *The Guardian of the Threshold*, and that in the soul of Maria there lives what had formerly been spoken.*

> ' Maria, as thou woulds't behold her, lives
> In other worlds than those where truth abides.
> My holy earnest vow doth ray out strength
> Which shall preserve for thee what thou hast gained.'

Now she says :

> ' In these clear fields of light me thou shalt find.'

She no longer says :

> ' In the cold fields of ice,' but†

> ' In these clear fields of light me shalt thou find
> Where radiant beauty life-power doth create ;
> Seek me in cosmic fundaments where souls
> Fight to recover their divine estate,
> Through Love, which in the whole beholds the self.'

* *The Soul's Awakening*, page 265.
† (*ibid*).

12

The words are turned differently from what they are in the first scene of *The Guardian of the Threshold*. Thereby what appears as a conversation between Lucifer and Benedictus :— ' I mean to fight,' ' And fighting serve the Gods,' becomes at the end of the tenth scene in *The Soul's Awakening* something quite different from what it was at the end of the third scene in *The Guardian of the Threshold*. Therewith light is thrown on something that like an Ahrimanic strain holds sway in all intellectual thought, in all the intellectual civilisation of the present day.

It is one of the most difficult things for the ordinary understanding faculty in modern civilisation to see that the same words in a different context mean something different. Modern civilisation is such that people think that when they have words, in so far as they are coined for the physical plane, they must always mean the same. Here we have precisely the place where Ahriman sits most firmly on men's necks—where he hinders them from understanding that words only become living in the deepest sense when one looks at them in the connection in which they stand. Nothing that reaches out beyond the physical plane can be understood if one does not keep this occult fact in mind. It is specially important for our present day that an occult fact of this kind should work upon our hearts, as a counterbalance to the external intellectual culture which has laid all men under its spell.

Further, among the many things that have to be considered in these Mystery Dramas, notice how the remarkable figure of Ahriman at first softly glides in just in *The Soul's Awakening* ; how it is seen, so to speak, insinuating itself between the personalities, and how it continually gains in significance towards the end of the play. I shall endeavour to bring before you in a special book such things as are to be noted for the delineation of Ahriman and Lucifer, and much else.*

It is no easy matter to get a clear understanding of such figures as those of Ahriman and Lucifer, and it may be specially useful perhaps to many, precisely in studying *The Soul's Awakening*, to pay a little attention to the fact that he who is not quite in a fog about the Ahrimanic element in the world, may think many a thing which perhaps another person through unconscious Ahrimanic impulses may be thinking too, but in another frame of mind. Perhaps there will be many among you, my dear friends, who can enter into all the circumstances which stream into such words as are expressed by Ahriman, so long as he is, so to speak, insinuating himself between the persons :†

*Note. This book—*The Threshold of the Spiritual World*—was produced during the course of these lectures.
† *The Soul's Awakening*, page 208.

13

'Let not thyself be quite confused by him,
He guards the threshold faithfully indeed,
E'en if to-day thou see'st him wear the clothes
Which for thyself thou did'st patch up before
Within thy spirit from old odds and ends.
Thou as an artist surely couldst produce
Thy actors in a better style than this ;
But thou will make improvements by-and-bye,
And e'en this clownish form can serve thy soul.
It doth not have to spend much energy
In showing thee that which it now still is.
Pay close attention to the Guardian's speech :
Its tone is mournful and its pathos marked,
Allow not this : for then he will disclose
From whom to-day he borrows to excess.'

I can quite imagine that many, from an aesthetic point of view, will find something blameworthy in the presentation of these Mystery Dramas. My dear friends, these objections also, among many others raised against Anthroposophy, disappear for those who can put themselves into the mood of Ahriman. The hypercritical people of the day who denounce Anthroposophy, belong entirely to those of whom the poet said : ' Folk do not note the devil even when he has them by the collar.' But we can judge of these opponents of Anthroposophy a little by what Ahriman here says while he is prowling round.

He meets us, however, in his more serious form where the death of Strader gradually comes into the events represented in the Mystery Dramas ; so comes it that the forces which proceed from this death must be sought for by the soul-vision in their effect upon all that happens besides in *The Soul's Awakening*.

It must be said, again and again, that this Awakening takes place in different ways. The way in which it happens to Maria is that through special circumstances those soul-forces which find their bodily-spiritual expression in Luna and Astrid appear before her soul ; the way in which it happens to Johannes Thomasius is that for him the magic web of his inner being is experienced as spiritually tangible (if one may use such an absurd expression), and appears before him in the other Philia ; and again in another manner to Capesius, through Philia. But this Awakening may gradually dawn upon souls, in a very different form, as we see it dawn in the eleventh scene for the soul of Strader. There we have not what we have already described as the spiritually-tangible soul-forces, Luna, Philia, Astrid, and the other Philia ; there we have still the imaginative pictures which pour spiritual experiences into physical consciousness. This stage of the Awakening of the Soul which took place thus in Strader can only be represented in such a way that an imaginative truth like the picture of the ship is represented. And in yet another form can the Awakening of the Soul be prepared. That you find again—and this purposely, after Ahriman has been shown in his deeper significance in the twelfth Scene,—you will find it indicated in the conversation between Hilarius and Romanus in the thirteenth scene. There the soul's vision has to be turned to what has been happening in the soul of Hilarius, from the events of *The Guardian of the Threshold*, to those in *The Soul's Awakening*, where this is expressed in the words of Hilarius : (*page* 279.)

> ' My friend, I thank thee for these mystic words.
> Oft have I heard them : now for the first time
> I feel the secret meaning they enfold.
> The cosmic ways are hard to comprehend—
> My portion, my dear friend, it is to wait
> Until the spirit points me out the way
> Which is appropriate to my sight.'

What are the words Romanus says ? They are those which Hilarius could always hear again and again from the place in which Romanus stands in the Temple—words that Romanus had often spoken in that place, and which up to this experience had passed before the mind of Hilarius without that deeper understanding which one may call understanding of life. It is already a part of the Awakening of the Soul when a person has pushed forward to an understanding of what he has taken in as thought-forms, and which he may have quite well understood and even lectured about, and yet does not possess as a living vital understanding. He may have taken in all that is made known by Anthroposophy, all that is contained in books, lectures, cycles, and may have imparted it to others perhaps to their great benefit, yet find that to understand as Hilarius understands the words of Romanus, is only possible after a certain experience for which he must calmly wait : a certain stage of the Awakening of the Soul.

Oh, if only a number of our friends could adopt this frame of mind, of awaiting the approach of something, which we have made known by means of theories and explanations which are perhaps apparently quite clear though still not understood, then perchance, something would also take effect in these souls of what is expressed in the third scene of *The Soul's Awakening* in the words of Strader. There, where Strader stands between Felix Balde and Capesius, where he stands between the two in such a remarkable manner, he stands there so that literally he hears every word they say and could repeat it all, but he cannot understand it. He knows what it is, and can indeed consider it to be wisdom, but now he remarks that there is such a thing as can be expressed in the words :*

> ' Capesius and father Felix both
> Conceal dark meanings in transparent words.'

Our supremely clever people of to-day will readily grant that ofttimes this or that person may chance to hide meaning, clear meaning, in obscure words ; but it will not be readily granted by one of these quite clever persons of the day that an obscure meaning can be hidden in clear words. And yet the concession that in clear words an obscure meaning may be hidden, is the higher of the two in human nature. Many sciences and many philosophies are clear ; but it would be an important thing if in the cosmic evolution of humanity philosophers would come to confess that, though from system to system in the philosophies, they had no doubt produced something clear and ever clearer, so that any one can say ' these things are clear,' yet, that there may be in clear words a hidden meaning ! If only many would learn—many who think themselves supremely clever and consider what they know (and in certain limits rightly so) as wisdom,—if they could only so place themselves before the world as Strader placed himself beside Father Felix and Capesius, and learn to say : †

> ' I often understood your present speech :—
> And then I thought it wise,—but not a word
> In all your speech can I now understand.
> Capesius and father Felix, both
> Conceal dark meanings in transparent words.'

Now, my dear friends, imagine to yourselves a philosopher of the present day or of the past, one who has evolved a philosophy, clear, and in its way plausible, and who takes his stand beside this philosophy of his (which philosophy is, in a certain sense, a result of the thought of humanity), and says : ' I often found what I had written was understandable ; I then considered it as

* *The Soul's Awakening*, page 188.
† (*ibid*).

16

wisdom ; and yet not a single word of what I said can I now understand ; in fact, in what I myself have written there is many a thing that is incomprehensible ; these words hide an obscure sense under clear words.' One cannot easily imagine such a confession coming from a philosopher either of the present or of the immediate past, nor from one of the very clever men in our materialistic, or, as we say, in more grandiose style, in our monistic age. And yet it would be a blessing for our present civilisation if people could assume the attitude towards the thoughts and other achievements of civilisation which Strader assumed to Father Felix and Capesius ; if only such persons might become more and more numerous, and if Anthroposophy could in very truth contribute something to this self-knowledge !

LECTURE 2

Munich, 25th August, 1913.

You will have seen that the experiences of the souls represented in *The Soul's Awakening* take place on the boundary between the sense-world and the super-sensible spiritual worlds. It is specially important for Spiritual Science that we should have well in our mind's eye this boundary region ; for it is only natural that at first all that the human soul can experience in the spiritual, super-sensible world, is in a way, an unknown land for all the faculties and all the psychic experiences of man in the physical sense-world.

Now, when a person has learned to accustom himself to the spiritual world through the various methods with which we have become acquainted, that is, when the soul learns to experience, to observe outside the physical body, then it is necessary for such life, for such experience in the spiritual world, that the soul should develop quite special faculties, quite special powers. When within its earth-existence the soul is striving after clairvoyant consciousness, it is natural that the soul that has either become clairvoyant, or is wishing to become so, should be able to stay in the spiritual world, without its body, and that it should be able to come back again into its physical body. It must, as an earth-being, be able to do this, and again live as a man, as a normal sense-being within the sense-world.

Thus we may say that the soul that has become clairvoyant must be able to move according to spiritual law in the spiritual world, and it must be able over and over again to step over the boundary between that and the physical world, and there—if I may express myself in everyday fashion—be able to behave correctly and sensibly. Since the faculties of the soul for the spiritual world, must be, and are, different from when the soul is employing the physical senses and all the rest of the physical body, the soul must, to a certain extent, if it wants to become clairvoyant, acquire mobility ; it must feel its way into the spiritual world, must have experiences there with the faculties that belong thereto, and then when it returns across the boundary it must again be able to experience the sense-world with the faculties corresponding to the latter. The

18

gaining of this adaptability, mobility, this faculty of transformation, is never easy. But if we are to estimate aright the difference between the spiritual world and the physically sensible world, we must keep clearly in mind just this boundary region between the two worlds. Precisely the Threshold must be kept well in mind, the Threshold over which the soul must pass when it wants to go out of the sense-world into the spiritual world ; for we shall see in the course of these lectures—and in many different ways—that it can only be injurious to the soul to carry the habits of the one world into the other when, in one direction or another, the Threshold has to be passed.

Our attitude when passing this threshold is specially difficult from the fact that within the constitution of our universe there exist those beings who play a certain rôle, as shown in the events represented in *The Soul's Awakening* and in the other dramas—the beings whom we may designate as Luciferic and Ahrimanic ; for in order to gain the correct relation already mentioned, in the transition from the one world to the other, it is necessary that we should know how to conduct ourselves aright towards both these kinds of beings, the Luciferic and the Ahrimanic. Now, in the first place, it would be easier—and this easy expedient is chosen by very many souls at least theoretically—to say : ' Well, Ahriman seems to be a dangerous fellow, and if he has such influence on the world and human actions, the simplest thing to do would be to eradicate from the soul of man the impulses that come from him.' This would appear to be the simplest, but to the spiritual world it would be about as sensible as if someone, in order to restore the balance to a pair of scales, were to take off the weight from the lower one. The so-called Ahrimanic and Luciferic beings are there in the world, they have their task in the universal order, and one cannot shut them out. Besides, it is not a matter of driving them out, but, as in the case of the weights on the two sides of the scales, the Ahrimanic and Luciferic forces must equalise each other, they must keep the balance in their influence on men and the other beings. We do not bring about the right activity of a force or of any kind of being by removing it, but by placing ourselves in the right attitude towards it. We have quite a wrong idea of these beings if we simply say that they are bad and harmful. That these beings in a certain sense rebel against the general order of the universe which had already been outlined before they entered into it, does not come about because they are bound under all circumstances to exercise a harmful activity, but from the fact that they—like the others with whom we must become acquainted as lawful members of the higher worlds—have a definite sphere of activity in the sum-total of the universe. Their resistance, their opposition to the cosmic order consists in their going beyond their sphere, they exercise beyond this sphere the

19

forces which they ought to employ only within their lawful domain. From this standpoint let us consider Ahriman or the Ahrimanic beings.

Ahriman can be well characterised if we say of him that in the widest circle he is the Lord of Death, the Ruler of all the powers which have to bring about within the physical world that which must of necessity be there, the destruction, the death of the beings within it. Death, in the sense-world, forms part of the necessary appointments, for the beings within it would soon overrun it if destruction and death were not present. The task fell to Ahriman of regulating this death aright and in the requisite manner from the spiritual world; Ahriman is the Lord of the ordering of death. In the most definite sense, the world of the minerals is the kingdom that falls to his share. The world is always dead; death is, so to speak, poured out over the whole of it. Furthermore, because our earth-world is constituted as it is, the mineral world and the laws governing it pervade all the other kingdoms of nature. Plants, animals, men, are all permeated, in so far as they belong to the realms of nature, by the mineral; they receive the mineral substances, and therewith also the forces and laws of the mineral kingdom, and are subject to the laws of the mineral kingdom in so far as the latter belongs to the being of the earth. Therewith, what justifiably belongs to death extends also into these higher domains of the lawful rule of Ahriman.

In that which surrounds us as external nature, Ahriman is the lawful Lord of Death; and in so far as he is this, he is not to be regarded as an evil power, but as one whose influence in the order of the universe is fully legitimate. We only enter into the right relation to the sense-world when we bring the proper interest to bear upon it, when the interest for this sense-world is so regulated that we see the things belonging to it come forth, and have not such a yearning after them as to demand eternal existence for the sensible forms, but can dispense with them when they meet with their natural death. To be able to rejoice aright in the things of the sense-world, but not to be so dependent on them that this would contradict the laws of decay and death, such is the lawful relation of man to the sense-world. In order that this may be so, in order that man may have a right relation to the sense-world, to growth and passing away,— for that reason he has the impulses of Ahriman within him, for that reason they pulsate through him.

But Ahriman can overstep his bounds: in the first place, he can so overstep them that he sets to work upon the thought of man. The man who does not look into the spiritual world and has no understanding for it, will not believe that Ahriman sets to work upon the thought of man in a quite real manner. But Ahriman does do this. In so far as this human thought exists in the sense-world it is connected with the brain, which, according to universal law, must fall into decay. Ahriman has to regulate the passage of the human brain towards decay. Now when he oversteps his domain, he then acquires the tendency, the intention, of loosening this human thinking from its mortal instrument, the brain. He tries to make it independent, to detach the physical thought, the thinking that is directed to the sense-world, from the physical brain into whose current of decay this thinking ought to be swallowed up when man goes through the Gate of Death. Ahriman has the tendency, when he admits man as a physical being into the stream of death, to snatch his thinking from this current of decay; throughout the whole of man's life Ahriman is always fastening his claws into this thinking, and he so works upon man that his thinking strives to escape from decay. Because Ahriman is thus active in people's thinking (and the men who are bound up with the sense-world naturally perceive only dimly the workings of the spiritual beings), those who are thus in the clutches of Ahriman feel the impulse to tear their thinking out of its proper place in the great cosmic order. This produces the materialistic frame of mind; this is the reason why men want to apply their thinking only to the sense-world. In most cases the persons who refuse to believe in a spiritual world are those who are obsessed by Ahriman, for it is he who attracts their thinking, and tempts it to remain in the sense-world.

For the mental attitude of a person the first result, if he has not become a practical occultist, is that he becomes just an unmitigated materialist and wants to know nothing about the spiritual world. It is Ahriman who leads him to this, only he does not notice it. For Ahriman, however, the matter stands thus: when he succeeds in severing this physical thinking from its foundation which is bound up with the brain, he sends out into the physical world shadows and phantoms which then pervade the physical world; with these Ahriman is continually endeavouring to found a special Ahrimanic kingdom. He is always standing on the watch when the thought of man wants to pass into the stream into which man will himself go when he crosses the door of death,—on the watch to snatch away as much as possible, to hold back the thinking, and to people the physical world with shadows and phantoms formed of physical human thought torn from its mother soil. Observed occultly, these shadows and phantoms glide about in the physical world disturbing the order of the world; they are products which Ahriman brings about in the way described. We have the right feeling towards Ahriman when we so estimate him that when he allows his lawful impulses to come into our souls we maintain a correct relation to the sense-world; but we must keep watch that he does not tempt us in the way indicated. Certainly that expedient which is employed by the people who say, ' Very well, we shall expel all Ahrimanic impulses from our souls ' would be more convenient. But by such an expulsion nothing would be attained except driving the other side of the scales right down. And whoever should succeed in driving out of his soul the impulses of Ahriman through a false theory, would fall into those of Lucifer.

This shows itself specially when people, out of a certain dread of the proper relation to the Ahrimanic powers, despise the sense-world and banish from within themselves joy in, and the right relation to, the sense-world, and, in order not to be attached to the latter, destroy all interest in it. Then comes in false asceticism, and this false asceticism offers in its turn the most powerful handle for the entrance of the unlawful Luciferic impulses. One could quite well write the history of ascetisicm by presenting it as a continuous allurement of Lucifer. In false asceticism a man exposes himself to the allurements of Lucifer, because instead of rightly balancing the scales and so using the forces polarically, he entirely empties one side.

Thus Ahriman's influence has its full justification in helping man to form a lawful estimate of the physical sense-world. The mineral world is Ahriman's very own kingdom, the kingdom over which death is poured out continuously. In the higher kingdoms of nature Ahriman is the Regulator of Death, in so far as he lawfully sets to work in the course of events and beings. That which is supersensible and which we can trace more in the external world, we designate for certain reasons as spiritual ; that which works more psychically in man, more in the soul or inner being of man, we designate as psychic. Ahriman is a more spiritual being, and Lucifer a more psychic being. Ahriman is, so to speak, the lord of that which takes place in external nature ; Lucifer presses forward with his impulses into the inner being of man.

Now there is also a lawful task belonging to Lucifer, one quite in accordance with the universal cosmic order. Lucifer's task is to prevent, in a certain respect, man and everything in the world pertaining to the soul, from merely living and being absorbed in the physical world. If there were no Luciferic power in the world, man would dream along in what would stream into him from the outer world as perceptions and in that which comes to him from the outer world through the intellect. That would be a kind of dreaming away of the human psychic existence within the sense-world. There are impulses which do not, indeed, tend to tear souls away from the sense-world in so far as they are bound up temporarily with the latter, but tend to raise them, so that they can live, feel and rejoice in a different way than they would through the sense-world alone. We need only think of what mankind has sought in the evolution of art. Wherever man creates in his life of imagination and feeling, something that does not cling grossly to the sense-world but rises above it, there Lucifer is the power which tears him away from the sense-world. A great part of that which is uplifting and emancipating in the artistic development of man is inspired by Lucifer. We can designate yet another thing as the inspiration of Lucifer. Through the fact that there are Luciferic powers, man is in a position not to remain dependent on the mere photographic imitation in thought of the physical sense-world ; he can raise himself in free thought above this. He does this, for instance, in his philosophising. From this point of view, all philosophising arises from Lucifer's inspiration. One could well write a history of the philosophic development of humanity, in so far as this is not pure positivism,—that is, in so far as it does not keep to the purely material,—and one might say, the history of the development of philosophy is a continual testimony to the inspiration of Lucifer ; for all creative work that rises above the sense-world we owe to the lawful forces and activities of Lucifer.

But now again Lucifer may overstep his domain ; and the resistance of the Luciferic beings to the cosmic order is always caused by their overstepping their domain. Lucifer oversteps and has the tendency continually to overstep it, when he infects the feeling-life of the soul. Whereas Ahriman has more to do with the thinking, Lucifer has more to do with the feeling and the life of the affections, the passions, the appetites and desires. Everything that can be psychically felt in the physical world is that whereof Lucifer is the Lord ; he has the tendency to detach and separate from the physical world this feeling-life of the soul, to spiritualise it and to set up, as one might say, in a specially isolated island of spiritual existence, a Luciferic kingdom composed of all he can seize of what is psychically felt in the sense-world. Whereas Ahriman wants to hold back the thinking in the physical or sense-world and make shadows and phantoms of it, so that it is visible to elementary clairvoyance as shadows gliding about, Lucifer does the opposite : he takes what is psychically felt in the physical world, tears it out and puts it into a special Luciferic kingdom that he is setting up in opposition to the general cosmic order, as an isolated kingdom similar to his own nature.

We can form an idea of how Lucifer can get at man in this way if we consider carefully a phenomenon in human life, about which we shall have to speak more in detail later on, the phenomenon which we designate as love in the widest sense of the word and yet which is really, properly speaking, the foundation of moral life in the human order of the world. Concerning this love in the widest sense, the following has to be said : When this love appears in the physical world and works within human life, it is absolutely protected from every unlawful Luciferic attack if its appearance is such that one person's love for another is for that other's own sake. When we are met by another being—another human being, or a being belonging to another kingdom of nature in the physical world, that being meets us with certain qualities. If we are freely receptive to these, if we are capable of being impressed by them, they then demand our love, and we cannot help loving this being. It calls forth the love in us. This love wherein the cause does not lie in the one who loves but in the one who is loved, this kind of love in the sense-world is absolutely proof against every Luciferic impulse. But now, when you observe human life, you very soon see that another kind of love plays its part in the life of man; that love in which a person loves because he himself has certain propensities which thereby feel pleased, delighted, satisfied. In this case he loves for his own sake; he loves because his natural disposition lies in a certain direction, and this special disposition finds its satisfaction in loving another being. He loves then for his own sake.

This love, which might be called an egoistic love, must also exist. It must not be lacking in humanity. For all that we can love in the spiritual world, the spiritual facts, all that love can cause to live in us as a longing for, as an impulse upwards to the spiritual world, to grasp the beings of the spiritual world, to recognise the spiritual world, also springs naturally from an egoistic love for the spiritual world, but this love for the spiritual must—not ' may,' but ' must '—be there, necessarily, for our own sake. We are beings who have our roots in the spiritual world. It is our duty to make ourselves as perfect as possible. For our own sakes we must love the spiritual world, so that we may draw as many forces as possible out of the spiritual world into our own being. In spiritual love this personal, individual element, what we might call this egoistic element of love, is fully justified, for it detaches man from the sense-world; it leads him up into the spiritual world, it leads him on to fulfil the necessary duty of making himself ever more and more perfect.

Now Lucifer has the tendency to mingle these two worlds one with the other; and wherever in human love, a person loves in the physical world with an admixture of egoism, for his own sake, this occurs because Lucifer wants to make physical love similar to spiritual love. He can then root it out of the physical or sense-world and lead it into a special kingdom of his own. So that all love that may be called egoistic love, that does not exist for the sake of the beloved but for that of the one who loves, is exposed to the impulses of Lucifer.

If we carefully consider what has just been said, we soon come to see that in modern materialistic civilisation, there is every reason to draw attention to these Luciferic allurements with regard to love; for a great part of our

24

present day outlook and literature, especially of the medical literature, is permeated with this Luciferic conception of love. We should have to touch upon a somewhat delicate subject if we wished to treat this more in detail ; but the Luciferic element in love is actually pampered by a great part of our medical science. When it is again and again said to men—for it is the male world that is specially pandered to here—that they must cultivate a certain kind of love because it is necessary for their health, that is, it is necessary for their own sake, —and much advice is given in regard to this matter, certain experiences in love are recommended to men which do not spring from a love for the other being, but because it is supposed to be necessary for the life of the male,—such instructions, be they ever so clothed in the garb of science, are nothing but inspirations of the Luciferic element in the world ; and Lucifer finds the best recruits for his kingdom among the men who allow such advice to be given to them and who can believe that it is necessary for the advancement of their own person to cultivate certain forms of love.* It is absolutely necessary to know such things, for stress must always be laid on what I said in the preceding lecture, that is, that people do not notice the devil, either in the Luciferic or the Ahrimanic form, even when he has them already in his clutches. People do not see that the person who, as a materialistic scientist, gives advice such as the above-mentioned is under the yoke of Lucifer ; they deny Lucifer because they deny all spiritual worlds.

Thus we see that on the one hand what is great and sublime, what carries and uplifts the evolution of humanity, is dependent upon Lucifer. Human beings must learn how to keep in their proper place the impulses which come from Lucifer ; for wherever Lucifer makes his appearance as the patron of that which is beautiful, as the patron of artistic impulses, something immense in humanity arises from the activity of Lucifer—something great and sublime. But there is also a shadow-side to Lucifer's activity. Everywhere Lucifer endeavours to tear away from the world of sense that which can be felt in the soul, to make it independent and permeate it with egoism and egotism. Thus there enters into that which is felt in the soul the element of self-will and similar factors, so that man forms for himself, with an unrestricted productivity, all kinds of ideas about the cosmos,—as one might say—with a free hand. How many persons indulge in speculative philosophy with the greatest ease, without troubling themselves in the least as to whether their speculations are in accord with the general necessary course of the cosmic order ! These eccentric speculators or ' cranks ' are really very widely distributed over the world; they are in love with their own ideas, they do not counterbalance the Luciferic

* At this time much harm was being done through the Theosophical Society by Leadbeater and others in this direction.

25

element with that of the Ahrimanic which must everywhere enquire whether that which man gains in the physical world by means of thought fits into the laws of the physical world. Thus we see these people going about the world with their ideas, these ideas being nothing but fantastic enthusiasm that does not fit in with the cosmic order. All such fantastic enthusiasms, all confusions of egoistic ideas, all eccentric opinions, all false, extravagant idealism, arise from the shadow-side of the Luciferic impulse.

When we examine into the conditions of clairvoyant consciousness we find that the Luciferic and Ahrimanic elements confront us with special significance on the border-land or threshold between the sensible and the supersensible. When the human soul has undertaken to do that which enables it to look into the spiritual world, it must then definitely undertake for itself the task which is otherwise carried out by the unconscious regulators of the soul's life. The general order of nature takes care that man does not in ordinary life transfer the customs and regulations of the one kingdom into the other too much, for this universal order of nature would get entirely out of control if the worlds were to be mixed up with one another. We have just laid stress on the fact that for the spiritual world love must evolve in such a way that a man must, above all, develop so as to be permeated with inner strength, he must develop the craving for self-improvement. He must have himself in view when he develops love for the spiritual world. If he transfers to that which is of the senses this same kind of impulse, which in the spiritual worlds can lead him to what is most sublime therein, it may then lead him to what is most detestable. There are persons who, in their external physical experience, in what they do throughout the whole day, have no special interest in the spiritual world. Such are by no means rare in our day. But nature does not allow of any ' ostrich-policy ' being used with regard to her. We know, do we not, that this ostrich-policy consists in the bird's sticking its head into the sand and then believing that the things it does not see are not there ? Now materialistically-minded people believe that, because they do not see the spiritual world, it is not there. They are real ostriches. But for all that, in their own soul, in the depths of that soul, the impulse towards the spiritual world does not cease to be, merely because they deny it, because they deaden themselves with regard to it. In every human soul, however materialistic, there is a living desire, a living love for the spiritual world. It is only that people make themselves unconscious of this impulse.

Now there is a law that what is repressed on the one side through being dulled, comes out on the other, and the consequence is that the egoistic impulse shoots into the sensual desires. The kind of love that is only in its proper place in the spiritual world shoots out from there, into the sensual impulses, passions and desires ; hence these sensual impulses become perverse. The perversity of the sensual impulses and all their horrible abnormalities, are the opposites of that which in the spiritual world would be lofty virtues, were man to use in the spiritual world the forces thus poured out into the physical world. At this point we must reflect that that which finds expression in the sense-world as loathsome impulses, could, if it were used in the spiritual world accomplish therein something of the most sublime character. This is of immense significance.

Thus you already see how, in this domain, the sublime is changed into the horrible when the boundary between the physical sense-world and the supersensible worlds is not properly observed and valued.

Clairvoyant consciousness must now so develop that the clairvoyant soul can live in the supersensible worlds according to the laws of those worlds ; it must be able to return again to the life in the body, without letting itself be led astray in the normal physical sense-world by the laws of the supersensible worlds. Suppose a soul could not do this, the following would then take place. (We shall yet see that the soul, in passing the boundary region between one world and the other, learns especially how to conduct itself aright, through meeting with the Guardian of the Threshold). Suppose a soul had made itself clairvoyant,—and that is a thing that may very well happen,—that through some circumstances or other it had become clairvoyant but had not gone through the meeting with the Guardian of the Threshold in the correct way. Such a soul could then see clairvoyantly into the supersensible worlds and could also observe things ; but it may happen that it then goes back into the physical world, and, not having been in the spiritual world in the right manner, it had only nibbled dainties in the spiritual world. Such eaters of sweets in the spiritual world are numerous, and it can truly be said that nibbling at the spiritual world is much more serious than it is in the sense-world. . . . Thus we see that one can nibble dainties in the spiritual world. And it very often happens that a person takes back into the sense-world what he has experienced in the spiritual world ; but then it densifies, it condenses. So that such a clairvoyant, that is, one who does not conduct himself according to the laws of the universal order, comes back into the physical world of the senses and brings with him the densified pictures and impressions of the spiritual worlds, and he no longer merely gazes at and thinks in the physical world, but, whilst living in his physical body, he has before him the after-effects of the spiritual world in pictures which are quite like the sense ones, only, that they correspond to no reality, they are illusions, hallucinations, dreamings, etc.

A man who can see aright in the spiritual world will never again confuse reality and fancy. Hence in the spiritual world, the philosophy of Schopenhauer, in so far as it is erroneous, refutes itself. In regard to its chief mistake it refutes itself even in the sense-world,—the mistake that all our environment is merely our imagination. When one tests this sentence it is already refuted in life when one is led to distinguish between a hot iron of 900 degrees which is really perceived, and the imaginary hot iron of 900 degrees, that causes no pain. Life itself reveals the difference if one lives in the real world with the capacities belonging to it; it readily reveals the difference between reality and fancy. The saying of Kant by which he formulated his so-called proof of God, that is, that a hundred imaginary dollars have just the same value as a hundred actual ones—that, too, is refuted by life. To be sure, a hundred imaginary dollars contain just as many cents as a hundred real ones, but for all that, there is a difference between the two which comes very strongly to the fore in real life. I would recommend everyone who considers that saying of Kant's correct, to try and pay his debt of a hundred dollars with imaginary ones; he would very soon notice the difference.

It is just the same in the physical world when one really stands within it and observes its laws, as it is also in the supersensible worlds. If one only nibbles, then one has no protection against the confusion of illusion and reality, for the pictures become dense and one takes what should be merely picture for reality. And the sweets a person has pilfered from the spiritual world are quite specially a booty which Ahriman can lay hold of. Out of what he can draw from ordinary human thinking, he gets only airy shadows, but, to use a commonplace expression, he gets quite plump shadows and phantoms when he presses out, as well as he can, the false illusory pictures from the individual human bodies, pictures that have arisen from this nibbling on the sly in the spiritual world. And in this Ahrimanic manner the physical world is filled with spiritual shades and phantoms which offer serious resistance to the general cosmic order.

Hence we can see how the Ahrimanic principle may very specially interfere, if it transgresses its boundaries and works against the general cosmic order; it can specially turn to evil, owing to the reversal of its legitimate activity. There is no absolute evil. Everything evil arises from the fact that what is in some way good is applied to some other use in the world and thereby is turned into evil. In a similar manner the Luciferic principle, which can lead to things so sublime and magnificent, may become dangerous, exceedingly dangerous, to the soul that has become clairvoyant. And that happens when the case is reversed. We have now considered the case in which a soul nibbles at the spiritual world, that is to say, when it perceives something there, and omits, on its return into the physical world, to say to itself : ' Thou mayest not now make use of the mode of thought which is suitable for the spiritual world.' For that soul would then be exposed in the physical world to the Ahrimanic influence. But the opposite may take place ; the human soul may carry into the spiritual world that which ought to belong only to the physical world, namely, the feelings and affections that the soul must of necessity develop in the physical world to a certain degree. None of the passions, et cetera, that the soul develops in the physical world, should be carried into the spiritual world, if that soul is not to fall a victim to the temptations and allurements of Lucifer.

We have endeavoured to represent something of this in the ninth scene of *The Soul's Awakening* in Maria's frame of mind and attitude of soul. It would be quite wrong for anyone to require in this scene something dramatically tumultuous and exciting, such as one has in an external physical drama. If the temperament of Maria were such that at the moment when she received the memories of the Devachanic world and of the Egyptian age her nature could have experienced exciting passions, impulses and emotions, her soul would have been dashed hither and thither by the waves of those passions. A soul that, in a state that is outwardly dramatic, cannot receive the impulses of the spiritual world with inner calm, in absolute tranquillity, suffers in the spiritual world a fate that I can only depict in the following pictorial manner. Imagine to yourselves a being made of rubber, and that this being was shot into a room enclosed on all sides, that it flew against one wall and was at once thrown back to the other, was then thrown back again, and thus flew hither and thither in a tumultuous movement on the waves of the life of passion. That actually happens to a soul which carries into the spiritual world the modes of sensation, feeling and emotion belonging to the physical world. But then comes something further. It is not agreeable to be thrown about in this indiarubber fashion, as if in a cosmic prison. Hence, in such a case, the soul, as a clairvoyant soul, follows the policy of the ostrich ; it stupefies itself regarding this state of being tossed hither and thither, it so deludes the consciousness that it notices nothing of it. It then believes that it is not being tossed hither and thither. Lucifer can then do all the more what he likes, because the consciousness is deadened ; he lures the soul out and leads it to his separate kingdom. There the soul may receive its spiritual impressions ; but they are purely Luciferic impressions, for they are received in his island-kingdom.

Because self-knowledge is difficult, and the soul attains only with extra-

29

ordinary difficulty to clearness regarding certain qualities, and because men have the desire to get as quickly as possible into the spiritual world, it is not to be wondered at that people say to themselves : ' I am already ripe, I shall undoubtedly control my passions.' Naturally, that is more easily said than done. Certain qualities are particularly difficult to get command of. Vanity, ambition and similar things, are so deeply rooted in the souls of men that it is not so easy to admit to oneself : ' I am vain, I am ambitious ! ' and in one's self-examination one generally deceives oneself just about these very things. These are the worst emotions. If a person carries them into the spiritual world he most easily becomes the prey of Lucifer. And then, because, when he notices that he is tossed hither and thither, he does not willingly say : ' That comes from vanity, from ambition,' he seeks to blind himself to the facts, and he is then carried off by Lucifer into his kingdom. There, certainly a person may have impressions ; but they do not coincide with the cosmic order which had already been planned, before Lucifer came on the scene ; they are spiritual impressions of a thoroughly Luciferic nature. He may have the most curious impressions and he will consider them to be absolutely correct truths. He may relate all sorts of incarnations of this person or that and these may be purely Luciferic inspirations and such like.

In order that the right conditions should come about on Maria's awakening, she had to be so represented, at the moment when the spiritual world was to rush in upon her with such force, that really to a person who might be quite a fine modern critic she must appear quite absurd. For a fine young critic of that kind might say : ' The Egyptian scene was taking place and there sits Maria, as if she had just come from breakfast, and she experiences these things in a way that lacks all dramatic feeling!' And yet anything else would be untrue at this stage of her evolution. This calmness alone represents the truth at this stage of her evolution, when the rays, the light of the spiritual falls upon the scene. Thus we see that it depends upon the soul's disposition, which must have mastered within itself all the emotions and passions which have significance for the physical world alone, if the soul is to cross aright the threshold of the spiritual world and is not to experience in the spiritual world the necessary consequence of what still remains of the mode of feeling pertaining to the senses.

Ahriman is a more spiritual being ; what he develops in the way of unlawful activity, of unlawful creative activity, flows, so to speak, into the whole of the sense-world. Lucifer is a more psychic being ; the soul-elements that have to do with feeling he wants to draw out of the sense-world and embody them in his special Luciferic kingdom, in which he wishes to ensure the greatest possibility of arbitrary independence to each man, according to the egoism implanted in the nature of the latter.

We see from this, that when we try to form a judgment of such beings as Ahriman and Lucifer, it cannot be a question of simply designating them as good or bad, but of grasping what is the lawful activity, the true domain, of these beings, and where their unlawful activity, the overstepping of their boundary, begins. For through the fact that they do overstep their bounds, they allure human beings to an unlawful overstepping of the boundary into the other world, with the faculties and laws of the one world. It is with what is experienced on passing to and fro across the boundary between the physical world and the super-sensible world, that the scenes in *The Soul's Awakening* have specially to do. In this lecture I wished to make a beginning by describing to you what must be carefully observed at the Threshold between the sensible and the supersensible worlds. In the following lecture we shall pursue the matter further.

LECTURE 3

Munich, 26th August, 1913.

In speaking about the spiritual worlds, as is being done in these lectures, it must be borne in mind that the clairvoyant consciousness which the soul of man may develop makes no difference to the nature and individuality of the person. For all that enters into this consciousness was already present in his nature. Because a person knows a thing he does not necessarily create it, he only learns to observe that which is already present as actual fact. Obvious as this is, mention must be made of it, because we must turn our thoughts to the fact that the nature of man lies in the hidden depths of existence and that it can only be brought up out of these depths through clairvoyant cognition. It follows from this that the real true nature of man's being cannot be brought to light in any other way than through clairvoyant consciousness. Through no kind of philosophy can we learn what man really is, we can only learn it through the kind of knowledge that is based on clairvoyant consciousness ; because, to the observation belonging to the sense-world and to the understanding connected with it, the being of man, the real, true nature of man, lies in hidden worlds. Now when this clairvoyant consciousness, from the point of view from which the worlds beyond the so-called Threshold are to be observed, first passes beyond this Threshold, in order that it may perceive and know, quite other demands are made upon it than are made in the sense-world. The chief thing is that the human soul is able to a certain extent to accustom itself to the fact that the way of looking at and perceiving things, which for the sense-world is the correct and healthy one, is not the only way.

Here I shall give the name ' the Elementary World ' to the first world which the soul of man, when it becomes clairvoyant, enters after having crossed the Threshold. Only he who wants to carry over the habits of the sense-world into the higher, supersensible worlds, can require that a uniform nomenclature shall be chosen for all the points of view from which the higher worlds are observed. (At the close of this course of lectures, and also in the brochure entitled *The Threshold of the Spiritual World*, I shall point out the connection that exists between the nomenclature here chosen—that is, in the designation ' elementary world,' and the designations 'soul world,' 'spirit world,' et cetera, used in my books *Theosophy* and *Occult Science*, so that people may not try, in a superficial manner, to seek for contradictions where such do not, in reality, exist).

The soul-life is met by quite new requirements when it passes over the Threshold into the elementary world. If the human soul desired to enter the elementary world with the habits of the sense-world, two things might happen : either cloudiness or complete darkness would spread over the horizon, over the field of vision of the consciousness : or else, if the soul had wanted to enter the elementary world without preparation for the peculiarities and requirements of the same, it would be thrown back into the sense-world. The elementary world is absolutely different from the sense-world. In the sense-world, when you pass from one being to another, from one process to another, you can then observe these beings, these processes ; but in front of every being, every process under observation, you distinctly preserve your own being, your own personality, enclosed within yourself. You know all the time that in the presence of another person or process you are the same person that you were, and that you will be the same when you confront a fresh one, and that you can never lose yourself in this process or that being. You stand before them,—you are outside them and you know that wherever you may go in the sense-world you remain the same. This becomes different immediately a person enters the elementary world. In this it is necessary that with the whole inner life of his soul he should so adapt himself to a being or to a process, that he transforms himself with his soul-life into this being itself, into this process. One can cognise nothing of a being or a process in the elementary world unless one becomes a different person within the being or process, and, indeed, in a high degree one similar to the being or process itself.

In the elementary world it is necessary to possess as a peculiarity of the soul the faculty of transforming our own being into foreign beings. We must have the capacity of metamorphosing ourselves. We must be able to immerse ourselves in and become the being itself, and if we wish to remain physically healthy, we must be able to lose the consciousness that is necessary for us in the sense-world—the consciousness : ' I am myself.' In the elementary world we only learn to know a thing if in a certain sense we inwardly ' become ' it. When one has crossed the Threshold one must so pass through the elementary world that with every step one changes oneself into each single process, and creeps, so to speak, into every being.

33

What in the physical world belongs to the health of a person's soul, namely, that in passing through the sense-world he holds his own in his very own being, that is quite impossible in the elementary world ; there it would lead either to the darkening of his field of vision, or to his being thrown back into the sense-world.

Now you can easily imagine that in order to exercise this faculty of transformation, something more is necessary than what we already possess in the sense-world. The soul of man is too weak to transform itself continually and adapt itself continually to each being, if it enters the elementary world as it is in the sense-world. The forces of the human soul must, therefore, be strengthened. Hence the necessity of those preparations described in my *Occult Science*, and in *Knowledge of the Higher Worlds and its Attainment*, which all lead to the soul's becoming stronger, more powerful in itself. It is then able to immerse itself in other entities without losing itself in the process. When such a thing as this is said, you see at once how necessary it is to take full notice of what is called the Threshold between the sense-world and the supersensible worlds. We have already said that clairvoyant consciousness, so long as the person exercising it is an earth-being, must continually pass to and fro, that it must make observations when outside the physical body in the spiritual world beyond the Threshold. It must then return into the physical body, and in a healthy manner exercise those faculties which lead to the right observation of the physical sense-world.

Suppose a consciousness that had become clairvoyant in the spiritual world were to take back into the sense-world this faculty of transformation which it must possess in order to be at all aware of a spiritual world. The faculty of transformation of which I have spoken is a peculiarity of the human etheric body, which lives chiefly in the elementary world. Now suppose a man were to return from the spiritual world into the sense-world, leaving this etheric body as capable of transformation as it has to be in the elementary world ; what would happen ? Each world has its particular laws, and is subject to them. The sense-world is the world of self-contained forms ; the Spirits of Form rule in the sense-world. The elementary world is the world of mobility, the world of metamorphosis, of transformation. When one wants to feel at home in the elementary world one must continually transform oneself, as all the entities of that world continually transform themselves ; there is no limited, enclosed form ; all is in continual metamorphosis. And a soul must take part in this metamorphosing existence outside the physical body, if it wants to live in the elementary world. In the physical sense-world we must allow our etheric body, which is an entity of the elementary world and capable of metamorphosis, to sink into the physical body. Through this physical body I am a definite person in the physical world ; I am this or that distinct person. My physical body stamps the personality on me, the physical body and the conditions of the physical world in which I am placed, make me a personality. In the elementary world I cannot be this kind of personality which requires a distinct form. But here we must note that what the clairvoyant consciousness recognises in the human soul is always present within it ; the mobility of the etheric body is only held together by the forces of the physical body. So soon as the etheric body sinks into the physical body its mobile forces are held together, they are adapted to that form ; but if the etheric body were not placed in the physical body as if in its case, it would have always the impulse to continual transformation.

Now suppose a soul that had become clairvoyant were to carry into the physical world in its etheric body this impulse for transformation, this etheric body with its tendency to mobility would then be, as it were, more loosely within the physical body ; and by this means a person, as human soul, would through the forces of his etheric body come into contradiction with the requirements of the physical world which desires to mould him to a definite personality. This contradiction arises because the etheric body, which desires free movement, if it comes back across the Threshold from the spiritual world to the physical world in the wrong manner, wishes every moment to be something else —which may place it in contradiction with the firmly imprinted form of the physical body. This may be expressed more precisely. In the physical body a man may be a European bank official, but because his etheric body has brought over into the physical world the impulse for getting free from the physical body—he may imagine himself the Emperor of China. Or to use another example, a person may be—let us say—the President of the Theosophical Society, and if her etheric body has become loosened, she may imagine that she has been in the presence of the Director of the Universe.*

Hence we see how in the most decisive manner attention must be given to the Threshold which sharply divides the sense-world from the supersensible world, how the soul must heed the requirements of each world, and adapt itself to these requirements, and how the soul must conduct itself differently according to whether it stands on this or the other side of the Threshold. That is connected with what must be repeated over and over again, namely, that the customs of the supersensible worlds must not be carried over unlawfully into the sense-world when one comes back across the Threshold. If I may be

* Leadbeater wrote that he had " stood with Mrs. Besant in the presence of the Director of the Universe." Mrs. Besant was at that time the President of the Theosophical Society.

35

allowed to speak quite plainly, I may say that one must understand how to conduct oneself properly in both worlds ; one may not carry over into the one world the method of observation that is right for the other.

Thus we have in the first place to note that the fundamental faculty for finding and feeling oneself at home in the elementary world is the faculty of transformation. But the human soul could not permanently live in this quality of being able to transform itself ; the etheric body could as little remain permanently in the elementary world in a state of being able to transform itself, as man in the physical world could remain continually awake. A man can only observe the physical world when he is awake : when he is asleep he does not perceive it. Nevertheless, he must allow the waking condition to alternate with the sleeping condition. Something similar is also necessary for the elementary world. Just as little as it is suitable for the physical world to be continually awake,—for life in the physical world must swing like a pendulum between waking and sleeping,—so is something similar necessary for the life of the etheric body in the elementary world. There must be an opposite pole, as it were, something that works in the opposite direction to the faculty of transformation which leads to perception in the spiritual world. What makes a man capable of transformation for the spiritual world is his life of 'imagination,' the faculty of making his ideas and thoughts mobile, so that through the thinking that has become mobile he can dip down into the entities and processes. For the other condition which admits of comparison with sleep in the sense-world, human volition must be developed and strengthened. Thus for the faculty of transformation, thinking or 'imagination' is required ; and for the other condition, will-power.

We shall understand what is meant here if we note that in the sense-world a man is a self, an ego, an ' I.' Through the fact that the physical body contributes what is necessary for this, when he is awake he feels himself a self, an ego. Such are the forces of the physical body that when a man dips down into it, it supplies him with the forces which allow of his feeling himself a self, an ego. This is not so in the elementary world. There it is the man himself who must carry out to some extent what the physical body accomplishes in the physical world. He can develop no feeling of self in the elementary world if he does not exert his will, if he does not himself do the ' willing.' That certainly does require a conquest of one's love of comfort, the love of the easy, the pleasant, which is so very deeply-seated. This self-willing is necessary for the elementary world ; and just as waking and sleeping alternate in the physical world, so must a condition of ' transforming oneself into other beings ' alternate in the elementary world with this feeling of self strengthened in volition. As

26

we become tired in the physical world through the work of the day, and our eyes finally close, in short, as after the day we are overcome by sleep, so do times come in the elementary world for the etheric body, wherein the latter feels : ' I cannot go on continually changing, transforming myself, I must now shut out all that is around me of other beings and processes ; I must now drive all that out of my field of vision and look away from all other beings and processes ; I must now will myself and live absolutely and entirely within myself and ignore the other beings and processes of the elementary world.' This willing of oneself, the excluding of other beings and processes, would correspond to sleep in the physical world.

Now we should picture things incorrectly were we to suppose that the alternation of the transformative faculty and of the strengthened ego-feeling were regulated in the elementary world in the same manner and with the same subjection to natural law as waking and sleeping in the physical world. For, as clairvoyant consciousness perceives,—and to this alone is it perceptible,— it takes place at will ; it does not pass over of itself as does waking into sleep, but after one has lived a shorter or a longer time in a state of metamorphosis, one feels the need within oneself of again experiencing and exercising, as it were, the other swing of the pendulum of elementary life. Thus, in a much more arbitrary manner than the waking and sleeping of the physical world, the transformative faculty alternates with living within one's self with a heightened feeling of self in the elementary world. Indeed, consciousness can, by its elasticity, bring it about that under certain circumstances both conditions can, as it were, synchronise ; so that on the one hand one transforms oneself to a certain extent and can yet keep together certain parts of the soul and rest within oneself. In the elementary world one can wake and sleep at the same time ; a thing that we should not exactly try to do for the good of the soul in the physical world ! Thus we see that in the elementary world there must also be an alternation in the soul's life, even as in the physical world waking and sleeping are necessary.

Further, when thinking develops the transformative faculty, when it begins to be at home in the elementary world, we must bear in mind that it cannot be used for the elementary world in the way that is quite right and healthy for the physical world. What, then, is this thinking in the physical world ? Try and follow up what it is. A man experiences thoughts in his soul ; he is aware that he grasps, produces, connects and separates these thoughts inwardly. Inwardly in his soul he feels that he is lord of these thoughts. They maintain a passive attitude, as it were, they allow themselves to be connected and separated, to be formed and again dismissed. This thought-life must in the elementary world develop a stage further. In the elementary world a man is not in a position to confront passive thoughts as he would in the physical world. If a man really succeeds in entering the elementary world with his clairvoyant soul, then it appears as though his thoughts were not things over which he has command, but they are living entities. Suppose your thoughts were not such that you could form and connect and separate them, but that in your consciousness each of them began to have a life of its own, a life as an entity. You put your consciousness, as it were, into something wherein you could not have thoughts as in the physical world, but wherein thoughts are living entities. I cannot do otherwise than employ a grotesque picture ; but this picture can help us to realise to some extent how different our thinking must become in the elementary world from what it is in the physical world. Suppose you put your head into an ant-heap and your thinking were to cease, and you had ants in your head instead of your thoughts. So when you dip down with your soul into the elementary world the thoughts become such that they of themselves connect with and separate from one another and lead a life of their own. Now, truly, we need a stronger force of soul in order to confront with our consciousness these living thought-entities than the passive thoughts of the physical world, which allow themselves to be formed at will, and which not only permit themselves to be connected sensibly and then separated, but often even quite foolishly. They are patient things, these thoughts of the physical world ; they allow anything to be done with them by the soul. When the soul plunges, so to speak, into the elementary world, that becomes quite different. There the thoughts live their own independent life ; there a man must stand up and assert his will over his soul-life, not confronting a passive thought-life but an active thought-life, possessing activity of its own. In the physical world we may actually think what is positively stupid, but as a rule that does not cause us pain. In the elementary world it may very well happen that when one does foolish things with one's thoughts, that which is creeping round as an independent entity may cause one real pain.

Thus we see that the customs of the soul-life must become quite different when we cross the Threshold from the physical into the supersensible world. If we were to pass over from the supersensible world, across the Threshold, and go back into the physical world with the habits that we bring to bear on the living thought-entities of the elementary world, and were then not to develop sound thinking with the passive thoughts, but wished to hold fast to the condition suitable for the elementary world, these thoughts would then continually run away from us, and we should pursue them, and become the slave of our thoughts.

If a man enters with clairvoyant soul into the elementary world and develops the faculty of transformation, then with regard to the inner life he dips down, plunges into it, transforming himself, according as he confronts this or that entity.

What, then, does he experience when he does this ? When he transforms himself into this or that entity, he experiences something that we might call sympathies and antipathies, which, as it were, well up from the depths of the soul, presenting themselves as experiences in the soul that has become clairvoyant. The sympathy or antipathy varies in nature, according as he transforms into one being or another. Whilst he thus proceeds from one transformation to another he continually experiences different sympathies and antipathies. And just as in the physical world a man characterises, describes, recognises, and in short, perceives objects and beings because the eye sees them in colours and because the ear hears them in sounds,—so correspondingly in the spiritual worlds he would describe its entities in particular sympathies and antipathies. But two distinct points are to be noted ; first, in speaking in the usual way in the physical world, we generally differentiate only degrees of sympathy and antipathy—stronger or weaker. This is not the case in the elementary world, for there the sympathies and antipathies not only differ from one another in degree, but also in quality, so that there are different kinds of sympathies and antipathies. As red and yellow are colours differing in quality so do the various sympathies and antipathies experienced in the elementary world differ in quality, the one is not merely stronger or weaker than the other. Hence in the elementary world it would not be a correct description if, following the custom of the physical world, we said that on plunging into one being we felt greater, and into another, less sympathy ; the sympathy differs in quality, as well as in intensity ; there are various kinds of sympathy.

That is one thing we have to notice. The other is that we cannot transfer into the elementary world the attitude towards sympathy and antipathy which is quite natural in the physical world. In the physical world we feel attracted by sympathy and repelled by antipathy ; we feel drawn to beings who are sympathetic to us and wish to be with them ; from beings and things that are antipathetic we turn away and will have nothing to do with them. As regards the sympathies and antipathies of the elementary world, it cannot be the case— if I may express it somewhat oddly—that the sympathies are sympathetic to us and the antipathies are antipathetic ; that cannot be in the elementary world. That would be just as if someone in the physical world were to say : I like only blue and green, but not red and yellow, I avoid these whenever I can. When in the elementary world an entity is antipathetic, this signifies that it has a distinct quality of the elementary world which must be described as antipathetic ; and we must behave towards what is there antipathetic to us as we do in the sense-world with regard to blue and red—not admitting one to be more sympathetic than the other. As in the physical world we meet all colours with a certain equanimity, because they express what the things are, and only if a man suffers from ' nerves ' does he run away from this or that colour, or a bull which cannot bear the colour red ; just as in the physical world we accept all colours with equanimity, so in the elementary world we should be able to observe with like equanimity sympathy and antipathy as qualities belonging to that world. For this it is necessary that the attitude of soul which feels itself attracted by sympathy and repelled by antipathy—which is quite natural in the physical world—must be changed to something quite different. That state of feeling, that frame of mind which in the physical world corresponds to sympathy and antipathy, must be replaced as regards the elementary world by what we might call soul-calm, spiritual peace. With an inwardly calm soul-life, a soul-life filled with peace of mind, must we immerse ourselves in the entities, and in so doing, whilst transforming ourselves into them, we must feel the qualities of these entities, rising within us as sympathies and antipathies. Only when we can do all this, when the soul can thus comport itself towards sympathies and antipathies, is that soul capable, in its experiences, of letting the feeling of sympathy or antipathy in the things of the elementary world pass in correct pictorial form before it. That is, only then are we in a position not merely to feel sympathies and antipathies, but really to see the experience of our own particular self transformed into another being, arising as this or that colour-picture, or this or that sound-picture of the elementary world.

You may also learn how sympathies or antipathies play a rôle in regard to the experience of the soul in the spiritual world if you read with a certain inner understanding the chapter in my *Theosophy* which treats of the soul-world. There you will see that the soul-world is entirely constructed of sympathies and antipathies and there one must meet them with equanimity.

From the description given above, you will have been able to see that what we know as thought in the physical world is really only the external, shadowy impress evoked through the physical body, of that thinking which exists in occult foundation and can be called a real living entity. As soon as we move in the elementary world with our etheric body, the thoughts become, as I might say, denser, more alive, more independent, more true in their nature. That which is experienced in the physical body as thought bears just the same relation to this truer element of thinking as a shadow on the wall to the object which casts it. In fact, it is the shadow of the elementary thought-life which is thrown into the physical world through the organisation of the physical body. When we think in the physical world our thinking is the shadow, as it were, of the thought-entities.

Supersensible, clairvoyant knowledge, therefore, opens out a view into the true nature of thought. No philosophy, no external science, no matter how ingenious it may appear, can give any correct pronouncement at all concerning the true nature of thought ; a cognition based on clairvoyant consciousness can alone know anything correct about it. And it is the same, too, with willing. The will must grow stronger, because in the elementary world things are not made so easy for us that the ' ego-feeling' can be called up through the forces of the physical body. There a man must himself desire and will this 'ego '-feeling, he must experience in the elementary world what it means to be entirely filled in the soul with the consciousness, ' I will myself,' and must experience as a most significant fact that the moment he is not strong enough to develop, not the thought, but the true act of will, ' I will myself,' he then finds himself becoming faint, as it were, unconscious. If he does not keep himself in hand in the elementary world, he then falls into a sort of fainting condition. There the true nature of volition can be perceived,—again, something that cannot be discovered by external science, or external philosophy, but only by clairvoyant cognition. What we call the will in the physical world is a reflection of that strong, living will of the elementary world which so develops that, out of its own volition, it maintains the self without support from external forces. We may say that everything becomes more voluntary in this elementary world, when we grow accustomed to it.

Above all, through the primal nature of the etheric body, when we have left the physical body and have in our etheric body the elementary world as environment, the impulse to transformation is aroused ; we wish to immerse ourselves in the entities. But just as in the course of our waking day-condition the need for sleep arises, so in the elementary world there arises in alternation with the impulse for transformation, the need of being alone, of shutting out everything into which one could transform oneself. Then again, when one has felt alone for a while in the elementary world, when one has for a while developed the strong volitional feeling, ' I will myself,' there comes what may be called a terrible feeling of isolation, a feeling of being forsaken, which evokes the longing again, to awake, as it were, out of this condition of willing oneself, to the faculty of transformation. In physical sleep we rest, and the forces take care that we awake without our doing anything towards it ; but in the elementary world, if we have transposed ourselves into the sleep condition of ' willing oneself only,' we are impelled to put ourselves again into the state of possessing the faculty of transformation (that is, of wanting to awake) through the call of the feeling of desolation.

From all this you see how different are the conditions of experiencing and feeling oneself in the elementary world from those of the physical world ; and you may judge how necessary it is again and again to take care that the clairvoyant consciousness which passes backwards and forwards from the one world into the other, really adapts itself properly to the requirements of the corresponding world, and on crossing the Threshold does not carry over the habits of the one world into the other. The strengthening and invigorating of the soul-life consequently forms part of the preparations often alluded to for the experiencing of the supersensible worlds.

Above all, those experiences of the soul which we might designate as the higher moral experiences, experiences which express themselves in the disposition of the soul as firmness of character, inner confidence and calm, must be strong and forceful. Inner courage and firmness of character must, above all, be developed in the soul ; for through weakness of character we weaken the whole soul-life and enter the elementary world with a weakened soul-life, which we should not do, for we should then be unable to have true and real experience in it. Hence, no one who is in earnest about the experiencing of the higher worlds will ever omit to lay stress on the fact, that to those forces which must strengthen the soul life so that it may rightly enter into the higher worlds, there belongs the strengthening of the moral forces of the soul. It is one of the saddest errors imposed on humanity if anyone ventures to say that clairvoyance may be acquired while the strengthening of the moral life is omitted. What I have described in *Knowledge of the Higher Worlds*, as the development of the lotus-flowers crystallising in the spirit-body of the clairvoyant, may indeed take place if the means for gaining moral strength have been omitted, but emphatically it ought not to do so.

These lotus-flowers must be there if a man wants to have the faculty of transformation ; for that capacity is brought about through the lotus-flowers developing their petals into motion outwards and away from him, and grasping the spiritual world, fastening themselves to it. What can be developed as the faculty of transformation expresses itself to clairvoyant vision in the unfolding of the lotus-flowers. What can be developed as the strengthened feeling of the ' ego ' is inner firmness, what we might call an elementary backbone. Both these must be correspondingly developed : the lotus-flowers so that one can transform oneself, and something similar to what is in the physical world a backbone, an ' elementary ' backbone, wherewith to develop one's strengthened ego in the elementary world.

Thus, as mentioned in the preceding lecture, that which, when developed in a spiritual manner, can lead in the spiritual world to virtues of a high order may, if allowed to stream down into the sense-world, lead to the most terrible vices. It is the same with respect to the lotus-flowers and the elementary spinal column. It is even possible that by practising certain methods one can awaken both the lotus-flowers and the elementary backbone without seeking moral firmness; but no conscientious clairvoyant would recommend this, for it is not merely a question of attaining this or that for the higher worlds, but that one should take heed of all that has to be considered.

The moment we cross the Threshold to the spiritual world we approach the beings of whom we have spoken, namely, the Luciferic and Ahrimanic beings, in a very different way from the manner in which we meet with them in the physical world. One remarkable thing is experienced as soon as we cross the Threshold. As soon as we have developed the lotus-flowers and the elementary backbone, we immediately see the Luciferic powers approaching, and their effort is to lay hold of the petals of the lotus-flowers. They stretch forth their tentacles towards our lotus-flowers, and we must have developed in the right way so that we make use of the lotus-flowers for grasping the spiritual processes, so that they are not seized upon by Luciferic powers. It is only possible to prevent their being seized by these powers if we ascend into the spiritual world with our moral forces strengthened.

I have already intimated that in the physical sense-world the Ahrimanic forces approach more from outside and the Luciferic forces more from within the soul. In the spiritual world it is just the reverse; there the Luciferic forces come from outside and try to lay hold of the lotus-flowers, while the Ahrimanic beings come from within and settle themselves firmly in the element-ary spine. Now, if we do not rise into the spiritual world well equipped morally, the Ahrimanic and Luciferic powers form a remarkable alliance with one another. If we have made our ascent filled with ambition, vanity, lust of power and pride, then Ahriman and Lucifer succeed in forming an alliance; I will employ a metaphor for what they do, but this metaphor expresses the truth. You will understand me when I say that what I hereby indicate really takes place. Ahriman and Lucifer form an alliance, and Lucifer and Ahriman together bind the petals of the lotus-flowers to the elementary spine, all the petals are fastened to the elementary backbone, and the man is imprisoned in himself, he is fettered within himself through his developed lotus-flowers and his elementary spine. The consequence of this is that egoism and love of deception enter and develop to an extent that would be impossible were he to remain merely in the physical world. This is what may occur if clairvoyant consciousness is

43

not developed in the requisite manner : Ahriman and Lucifer form a compact, by means of which the petals of the lotus-flowers are fastened to the elementary spinal column, and thus a man is imprisoned within himself through his own elementary or etheric faculties. These are all things that we must know, if we wish to penetrate with open eyes into the real spiritual world.

LECTURE 4

As the soul that has become clairvoyant progresses further and further, it forges its way out of what we have in these lectures called the elementary world, and enters into the really spiritual world ; and much of what has been already indicated must be still more carefully attended to when it is a question of the ascent of the human soul into the actual spiritual world. Within the elementary world, in the affairs and phenomena which therein surround the soul that has become clairvoyant, there is still much that reminds it of the qualities and forces and all sorts of things in the physical or sense-world ; but when the soul rises into the spiritual world, it encounters the qualities and characteristics of the phenomena and the various beings, in quite another manner from what was the case in the sense-world. In the spiritual world the soul must to a greatly increased extent, disaccustom itself from wishing to manage with the qualities, powers and views which suffice for the sense-world. It is most disturbing to the soul when it has to confront a world to which it is totally unaccustomed, a world which necessitates its leaving behind, as it were, all that it has so far been able to experience and observe. Nevertheless, if you keep in mind my *Theosophy*, or *Occult Science*, or the fifth and sixth scenes of *The Soul's Awakening*, in which representations of the real spiritual world are given, it will occur to you that all these representations, the more scientific ones as well as those that are more pictorial and of scenic effect, are given in illustrative material, taken from the impressions and observations of the physical or sense-world.

Recall for a moment how the passage through Devachan is presented to you, or, as I have called it, the passage through the Spirit-land. You will find that the pictures there employed contain characteristics taken from the physical outlook. As a matter of course, when one undertakes to give on the stage a scenic presentation of the region of spirit,—the region which the human soul experiences between death and a new birth,—then it is necessary to characterise the phenomena and everything that takes place, in pictures taken from the physical sense-world. For you can easily imagine that the stage-hands

45

of to-day would have little idea what to do with something taken from the spirit-world, if it had nothing in common with what exists in the sense-world. Thus, one is under the necessity in representing the spiritual world of expressing it by means of pictures taken from physical observation. But that is not all. It might easily be thought that in giving the representation one must proceed so that what is represented by a physical picture only points to a world that, in its characteristics, has nothing in common with the sense-world. It might easily be believed that one who wishes to represent this world would simply be obliged, in order to help himself out of the difficulty, to have recourse to pictures from the physical world. That is not however the case ; for the soul which has become clairvoyant, when it withdraws into the spirit-world, really sees the scenery exactly as shown in those two scenes. They are not just imagined in order to give the characteristics of something quite different, for the soul that has become clairvoyant is really in such scenery, and is surrounded by it. As in the physical sense-world the soul is in the midst of a landscape wherein are rocks and mountains, woods and meadows, and as when the soul is sound and healthy these are considered as reality, so the soul, that has become clairvoyant when it is outside the physical and etheric body, is surrounded in exactly the same way by scenery which is made up of these pictures. They are not chosen arbitrarily, but in the world we are considering, they really are the actual environment of the soul. Thus it is not as though the fifth and sixth scenes in *The Soul's Awakening* had come into existence because something pertaining to an unknown world had to be expressed and one thought something out for this purpose, but it is a fact that the world thus depicted is all round the soul and it merely depicts to some extent what it sees.

Now it is also necessary that the soul that has become clairvoyant should obtain the right relationship to the true reality of the spirit-land, which has nothing in common with the sense-world. An idea of this relationship, which the soul must acquire to the spiritual world, may be obtained if we try in the following way to describe the manner in which the soul has to comprehend the spiritual world. Suppose you open a book and that at the top you find something like a dash from left above, to right below, then a stroke from left below to right above, then again a stroke from left above to right below, parallel to the first, and another from left below to right above, parallel to the second ; then comes something that is like a circle above, and below there is a circle that is not quite closed ; then comes something that has two vertical strokes joined together above and the same again. You do not do all this when you open a book and look at the first thing you find there, do you ? You read the German word, ' wenn.' You do not describe the ' w ' as strokes, and the ' e ' as a circle above and a not quite closed circle below, etc., but you read. When you look at the forms of the letters before you, you obtain a relationship to something that is not impressed on the page of the book, but is indicated to you by that which is on the page.

It is precisely the same with the relationship of the soul to the whole picture-world of the region of the spirit. What a person has to do there is not merely to describe what he sees; it is more like reading; what he has in pictures before him is in reality a cosmic writing, and he acquires the correct inner attitude towards it if he feels that in the pictures he sees a cosmic writing, and the pictures impart that which is the reality of the spiritual world, of which this whole picture-world is actually woven. Hence in a real, true sense, we must speak of a reading of the cosmic writing, in the region of spirit.

It should not however be imagined that this reading of the cosmic script can be learnt like reading in the physical world. Reading in the physical world to-day is grounded more or less (though in the primitive ages of humanity it was not so) on the relation of arbitrary signs to that which they signify. Such a learning as is necessary for reading these arbitrary signs is not required for the cosmic writing, which presents itself as a mighty tableau, as the expression of the spiritual world to the soul that has become clairvoyant. Rather ought one simply to receive impartially and with receptive soul that which is shown there as picture-scenery; for that which is experienced thereby is really reading. The meaning of these pictures flows out of the pictures themselves, so to say. Hence it may easily happen that any sort of comment or interpretation of the pictures of the spiritual world in abstract ideas may be far more of a hindrance than a help to lead the soul to what lies behind the occult writing.

In a case of this sort, as well as in my book, *Theosophy*, and again in the scenes in *The Soul's Awakening*, it is, above all, a matter of letting things work impartially upon one. In the deeper forces, which oft-times come quite phantom-like to one's consciousness, one already experiences a foretaste or an indication of the spiritual world. In order to obtain this it is not at all necessary to strive after becoming clairvoyant—bear this well in mind; for in order to understand such pictures it is only necessary to keep one's mind receptive to them, not approaching them with a coarse materialistic attitude, saying, ' this is all nonsense, there are no such things.'

A receptive soul following the course of such pictures soon learns to read them. Through the devotion of the soul to such pictures there results the requisite understanding for the world of the spirit. Because what I have said is really a fact, the numerous objections to Spiritual Science, which are the result of the materialistic outlook of the day, can be explained. Such objec-

47

tions are really on the one hand very obvious, and on the other they may be very clever, and apparently very logical. They can be made in the following manner. A person may say—and this objection is really not unjustifiable—like Ferdinand Fox (or Reinecke) in the play, who is so supremely clever that he is not only considered so by men, but also quite properly by Ahriman himself—he may say, ' Yes, you who describe to us the clairvoyant consciousness, you who speak to us of the spiritual world, you nevertheless compose all this world simply by means of the material of sense-ideas ; you group together the material of sense-ideas. How can you maintain that from this we are to experience something new, something we cannot experience unless we approach the spiritual world, seeing that you really only put together a scenery composed of known sense-pictures ? ' That is an objection that must confuse many, and which, from the standpoint of present-day consciousness, is made with a certain apparent, and, indeed, even with full justice. And yet when one goes more deeply into such objections as those of Ferdinand Fox, the following is correct : such an objection would be very like one which a man would make to someone who has received a letter : ' Yes, you have received a letter, but I see in it nothing but letters and words, which I have known for a very long time. How are you going to learn anything new from that ? You can only get something from it which we all know already ! ' And yet, under some circumstances, we get to know by means of that which we have known for ever so long, something that could not have entered even into our dreams. Thus it is also with the picture-scenery, which must not only appear on the stage, but be everywhere manifest to the clairvoyant consciousness. In a certain way it is composed of reminiscences of the sense-world ; but when it presents itself as cosmic script, it represents that which man cannot experience either in the sense-world or in the elementary world. Stress must always be laid on the fact that this attitude towards the spiritual world must be compared to reading, and not to direct contemplation.

Thus, whereas the earthly man who has become clairvoyant has to grasp the things and phenomena of the sense-world (if he wants to maintain his healthy attitude of soul to these things) in such a way that he looks at them and describes them as exactly as possible, his relation to the spiritual world is a different one. There, so soon as we cross the Threshold into the spiritual world, we have to deal with something that must be compared with reading. If we bear in mind what has to be recognised for human life from this land of the spirit, there is certainly something else that can defeat the objections of Ferdinand Fox. Such objections are not to be taken lightly ; if we want to understand Spiritual Science aright we must come to an understanding about them. We must remember that in great measure the men of our day cannot help making objections, because their ideas and habits of thought are such that from dread of being confronted with nothingness, when they hear of the spiritual world, they simply reject it. We can form quite a good idea as to their attitude towards the spiritual world if we observe what is thought about the spiritual world by men who really, in a certain sense, are well-intentioned towards it.

Recently a book has appeared which those who have already gained a real understanding for the spiritual world may find it worth while to read ; it is the work of a man who is really well-intentioned and who would very willingly construct for himself some sort of knowledge of the spiritual world. The book is called, *Concerning Death*, by Maurice Maeterlinck. It is the work of a man who shows in the very first chapters that he would like to understand something of these matters ; and his example is of quite special interest, for we know that, in a certain way, he is a man of fine discernment, who has allowed himself to be influenced by Novalis, among others ; that he has, in a way, specialised in mystical romance, and that he has himself accomplished much that is very interesting, both in theory and art, in regard to the relation of man to the super-sensible world.

In the chapters in which he speaks of the actual relation of man to the spiritual world, his book becomes quite foolish and absurd. It is an interesting phenomenon that this man, who is well-intentioned but works with the habits of thought of the present time, becomes absurd. I do not say this in order to indulge in rude criticism, but in order to show objectively that a man of such good intentions may become absurd when he wishes to grasp the relation of the human soul to the spiritual worlds. For Maurice Maeterlinck has not the least idea that there is a possibility of the human soul being so strengthened and fortified that it can leave behind it all that can be attained through sense observation and ordinary thinking, feeling and willing, on the physical plane, and indeed, even on the elementary plane. To such minds as Maeterlinck, when the soul leaves behind it all that composes sense-observation and the thinking, feeling and willing that are therewith connected, there is simply nothing left. Hence, in this book, Maurice Maeterlinck demands proofs of the spiritual world and its facts. Naturally, it is quite justifiable to demand proofs of the spiritual world. We have every right to do so, but not in the way that Maeterlinck does. He would like to have proofs that are as palpable as the proofs given by science for the physical plane. And, because in the elementary world things are still reminiscent of the physical world, he would even be satisfied to be convinced of the existence of spiritual things, by means of experiments which are copies of the physical ones. That is what he demands. Thereby he shows that he has not the very smallest understanding of the true spiritual world ; for he wants to prove, by means borrowed from the physical world, things and processes which have nothing to do with the things and processes of the physical world. Rather should it be one's task to show that such proofs as those demanded by Maeterlinck are impossible for the spiritual world.

I must ever and again compare such a demand as that of Maeterlinck with something that has taken place in mathematics. Up to quite recent times the various academies were frequently receiving treatises concerning the so-called squaring of the circle. People were trying to prove geometrically how a circle may be changed into a square. Innumerable mathematical treatises with mathematical demonstrations have been written on this subject. To-day only a mere amateur would attempt to write such a treatise, for it has been proved that such a squaring of the circle by geometrical means is not possible. Now what Maeterlinck demands as proof for the spiritual world is, transferred to the spiritual sphere, nothing but the squaring of the circle, and is just as much out of place for the spiritual world as is the squaring of the circle for mathematics.

What is it that Maeterlinck really demands ? If we know that as soon as we cross the Threshold to the spiritual world we live in a world that has nothing in common with the physical nor yet with the elementary world, we cannot then make the demand : ' If you want to prove anything you must please go back into the physical world and there prove to me the things of the other, the spiritual world.' With respect to the things of Spiritual Science, we must face the fact that absurdities are committed by the most well-meaning people, and when these things are transferred to ordinary life they at once appear absurd. It is as though someone were to say that a man ought to stand on his head and yet continue walking on his feet. If a person were to demand that, everyone would see that it was nonsense ; but when this is done in regard to proofs of the spiritual world, it is considered clever, it is a scientific demand ; its author is the last one to notice its absurdity, and his followers naturally do not remark it either, especially if the author is celebrated. The whole fault of such demands springs from the fact that the persons who make them have never clearly grasped man's relation to the spiritual world.

When, by means of clairvoyant consciousness, we obtain concepts that can only be acquired in the spiritual world, these may naturally meet with much opposition from people like Ferdinand Fox. All ideas which we are to acquire concerning so-called reincarnation, that is, real reminiscence of earlier earth-lives, can only be gained by means of that attitude of the soul which is necessary towards the spiritual world, for such can be obtained from the spiritual world alone. Now when one has in one's soul impressions and ideas which refer one back to earlier earth-lives, such impressions are specially exposed to the opposition of our present age and from the outset it should, of course, not be denied that the worst nonsense is carried on in this domain ; for many people have various impressions and refer them to some preceding incarnation. It is then very easy for the opponent to say, ' What flows into your soul-life are recollections of experiences you have had between birth and death, only you do not recognise them as such.' One must acknowledge the fact that it may be so in many hundreds of cases ; but we should clearly understand that the spiritual investigator must be thoroughly well acquainted with such matters. It may quite well be that someone experienced something in his childhood or youth and that at a later stage of life what had previously been experienced comes back again into his consciousness, but completely transformed. It may be that he does not recognise this and looks upon it as a reminiscence of a previous incarnation or earth-life. That can be the case. We know well enough within our own circle how easily it may occur. You see, memories may be formed even about that which a man has not clearly experienced ; he may have an experience that flits by so quietly that while it is happening he has no clear consciousness of it, and yet it may reappear later as a memory and may then be quite clear. Hence, if he is not sufficiently critical with himself, he will swear that this is something in his soul that he has never experienced in this present life. Because this is so we can understand that much mischief has been done by people who have busied themselves, though not earnestly enough, with Spiritual Science. This may occur precisely about the doctrine of reincarnation, since, in regard to this, so much of human vanity and human ambition has to be taken into consideration. To many people it is a thing greatly to be desired that in a previous incarnation they should have been Julius Cæsar or Marie Antoinette. I could, for example, count as many as twenty-five or twenty-six Mary Magdalenes I have met in this life ! In this domain so many things play a part and give rise to mischief, that the occult teacher has reason to make himself aware of the mischief wrought in this connection. Something else must, however, be emphasised with regard to this subject.

In true clairvoyance, when there are impressions of previous earth-lives, these impressions appear with a certain characteristic, which if the clairvoyant has a healthy soul he can very clearly recognise and know unmistakably that it is not connected with anything arising from the present life between birth and death. For these reminiscences, these real and genuine memories of earlier earth-incarnations that come from true clairvoyance, have something too striking and surprising to allow one to believe that the soul could bring them out of its depths by any means humanly possible ;—unless it were helped, not only by what is in its conscious, but also by what is in its subconscious depths. As students of Spiritual Science we must acquaint ourselves with that which a soul may meet with as the result of its external experiences. It is not merely the wishes and desires (which do, indeed, play a great part when impressions are brought up from the unknown depths of the soul in a changed form, so that one does not recognise them as experiences of the present life) ; there is an interplay of many other things. But those things which are as a rule the overpowering impressions coming from a previous life on earth can be very easily distinguished from impressions which come from the present life. To mention an example : If someone has a true impression of a former earth-life, he will then, as a rule, inwardly experience the following, as if it arose from the soul-depths : ' You were such and such a person in the previous earth-life.' And then, at the time when this impression comes, it will be found that, externally, in the physical world, he can make no use of this knowledge. It may bring him forward in his evolution, but as a rule he says to himself, ' Now, in your previous incarnation you were gifted with this or that faculty ; ' but by the time that such an impression comes, he is already too old to do anything with what he was in the previous incarnation. There will always be circumstances to show that these impressions cannot possibly arise from what might come from the present life ; for if he were to work out from what he fancies, he would attribute to himself quite other qualities when constructing his former incarnation. As a rule, a person does not allow himself even to dream what he was like in a preceding incarnation. It is generally very different from what we think and if we have an impression that we had a certain relation to some person on earth,—which in true clairvoyance arises as a real and correct impression of a preceding earth-incarnation—even then the fact must be remembered that in incorrect clairvoyance so many previous incarnations have been described in the same way, in relation to friends and foes whom one has in one's immediate surroundings. These conjectures are mostly nonsense. If a really correct impression comes, it is seen that one has a relation to a person with whom it is impossible to come into touch when one receives the impression, showing how impossible it is to apply these things to direct practical life.

With regard to such impressions we must also develop the disposition that is necessary for clairvoyant consciousness. Naturally, when one has the impression : ' I stand in such and such a relation to this person ; the things, of which an impression is received, must be worked out in life ; one must again

52

come into relationship with the person.' But that may only come about in a second or third earth-life. One must have a feeling of being able to wait quietly, a feeling that may be designated as real inner peace of soul, peacefulness of spirit. This is the right way of judging what one experiences in the spiritual world.

If we want to learn something about some person or other in the physical world, we may then do whatever we may consider necessary for the purpose : but we cannot do so unless under the impression of spiritual peace, calmness of soul and being able to wait. It is absolutely a correct description of the right disposition of the soul towards the true impressions of the spiritual world which says : ' Strive after nothing, only wait quietly and peacefully, the inner being of the soul in a state of calm expectancy.' In a certain respect this feeling must be poured out over the whole soul-life, if the clairvoyant soul is to approach aright the experiences of the spirit-land.

The ' Ferdinand Fox,' however, is not always so easy to refute, even in a case when impressions arise in the soul of which one might say : It is not human-ly possible that the soul with the forces and habits which it has acquired in the present earth-life should imagine what rises out of its depths ; on the contrary if it depended on these qualities the soul would have imagined something different. Even when one can say something that is a sure sign of the real, true impressions of the spiritual world, a super-clever Ferdinand Fox may come and raise objections. In occult science one must take the standpoint that with regard to the objections made by those who are far removed from occult science, and also by opponents, who do not want to know anything about it, one does not say : ' The whole inner life of the soul is filled with expectation.' With regard to the spiritual world that is the correct frame of mind, but in regard to the objections of the opponents one should not, as an occult investigator, remain merely in expectation, but should oneself seriously raise all these objections, so that one may know what objections can be raised. And there is one obvious objection which is also made in the psychological, psycho-pathological, physio-logical literature, and frequently in the treatises that pass as learned and scientific ; the objection is this : ' The psychic life of man is very complicated ; in its depths there is much that does not penetrate into the upper consciousness ; not alone do the wishes and desires bring out all sorts of things that are beneath in the depths of the soul.' Thus does a person speak nowadays when he wants to be very smart and he says : ' The soul-life is indeed so complicated that when it has an experience of any kind it experiences in secret something like a resist-ance, a kind of opposition to that which it experiences. Concerning this opposi-tion which the person always experiences, he, as a rule, knows nothing ; but it can push its way from below into the upper regions of the soul-life.' Things are often admitted in the psychological, psycho-pathological, physiological literature, because the facts cannot be denied—things like the following: ' When a soul is thoroughly in love with another, it cannot do otherwise than develop in the unconscious soul-depths, side by side with the conscious love, a fearful antipathy against the beloved soul.' And the view of many a psycho-pathologist is that if anyone is thoroughly in love with another, in the depths of that soul there is real hatred. This hatred is only over-powered by the conscious passion of love, but yet hatred is present.

Then, say those like Ferdinand Fox: ' when such things come up from the depths of the soul, these are impressions which may very easily present the illusion that they cannot have their seat in the individual soul in question ; and yet they may be experienced, for the soul-life is complicated—' so says Ferdinand Fox. We can only reply : Certainly ; that is as well-known to the spiritual investigator as it is to the modern psychologist, or psycho-pathologist, or physiologist. The making of such objections is deeply rooted in the materialistic consciousness of our times. We realise this when we go through the above-mentioned literature of the day,—literature dealing with the soul-life in its condition both of sickness and of health. We have impressions that Ferdinand Fox is a realistic figure, everywhere apparent, an extremely import-ant figure in the present day. He is no invention. When one takes, page by page, all the writings that appear so abundantly everywhere, one has the im-pression, on turning the pages, that the remarkable face of Ferdinand Fox springs out at us everywhere. He pervades the whole scientific literature of the day, but with regard to him one must emphasise again and again—and I do not scruple, with regard to him, to repeat one thing again and again—one must repeatedly emphasise that the proof that a thing is no fancy but actuality and reality, must be given by life itself. Again and again 1 must repeat that the part of the philosophy of Schopenhauer, in which he takes the world as if it were only imagination, and as if it were not possible to distinguish imagination from real perception, can only be contradicted by life itself ; even as the declara-tion made by Kant with respect to the so-called proof of the existence of God, that a hundred imaginary shillings contain as many pence as a hundred real shillings, can be contradicted by every one who would like to pay his debts with imaginary shillings and not with real ones. And that, too, which is called pre-paration for, or accustoming oneself to, clairvoyance, must be taken in its reality. It is not merely a case of theorising, but of accustoming oneself to a life by means of which we can distinguish in the realm of spirit, just as clearly a true impres-sion of a preceding earth-life from one that is not true, as when laying a hot iron on the skin we can distinguish that from one that is purely imaginary. When we reflect on this, we shall also clearly understand that the objections of Ferdinand Fox really mean nothing at all in this domain, because they come from people who—I will not say, have not entered the land of spirit clairvoyantly, but—have never even understood it.

Thus it must be kept in mind that when we cross the Threshold of the spiritual world we enter a region of the universe which has nothing in common with that which the senses observe, or with what we experience in the physical world through willing, feeling and thinking. We must also approach the peculiarities of the spiritual world by realising that the ways and means whereby we observe in the physical world must be left entirely behind us. In referring to the mood of perception in the elementary world I employed a simile that may have appeared grotesque—that of putting one's head into an ant's nest. But so it is with the consciousness in the elementary world. There we have not to do with thoughts that put up with everything, that hold themselves passive, but rather do we put our consciousness into a world, into a thought-world, if one likes to call it such, which creeps and crawls, having a life of its own. Hence a man must hold himself firmly upright in his soul against the thoughts which move of themselves. But in the elementary world many a thing, even in this realm of creeping, crawling thoughts, still reminds us of the physical world.

When we enter into the true spiritual world there is no longer anything which reminds us of the physical world, but there we enter into a world for which I shall employ the expression I have also used in my work, *The Threshold of the Spiritual World,*—a world of living thought-beings. In this spiritual world we find that of which, when we think in the physical sense-world, we have only something like silhouettes, thought shadows ; we find the thought-substance of which the beings consist into whom we transfer and transform ourselves. As human beings in the physical sense-world consist of flesh and blood, so do these beings in the spirit world consist of thought-substance ; they are thoughts, simply thoughts, nothing but thoughts, yet living thoughts with an inner essential being ; they are living thought-beings.

Hence these thought-beings into which we enter cannot accomplish actions such as we perform with physical hands. What the beings accomplish as action which brings about the relation of the one being to the other, can only be compared in the spiritual world with that which exists in the sense-world as a weak reflection of it in the embodiment of the thoughts in speech. We accustom ourselves to live in the spiritual world, we experience living thought-entities ; and all that they do, all that they are and the way in which they

55

affect one another, forms a spirit-language. One spirit speaks to the other ; a language of thought is spoken in this spirit-land ! But this spirit-language is not merely a language, for as a whole it represents the deeds of the spirit world. When these beings speak, they act, they have dealings together, they are active.

Thus when we cross the Threshold into the spiritual world we become familiar with a world wherein thoughts are beings and beings are thoughts, but these beings are much more real there than are men of flesh and blood in the sense-world. We enter a world in which action consists of spirit-speech, where the words move hither and thither and where, whenever something is spoken, it takes place. Hence of this spiritual world and of the occurrences within it we must say, as is said in the third Scene of *The Guardian of the Threshold* : 'Here in this place words are deeds, and other deeds must follow these.' All occult perception and everything that the Initiates of all times have accomplished for humanity, show in one special domain what this spirit-speech, which is at the same time spirit-action, signifies ; and with a characteristic expression it was called the Cosmic Word.

We now see that our study has brought us directly into Spirit-land ; and the Beings and the acts of those Beings confront us ; and their sum-total is the many-voiced, many-toned Cosmic Word, rich in manifold activities—the Cosmic Word in which we become accustomed to live with our own resounding psychic being, ourselves Cosmic Word, so that we ourselves perform deeds within the spiritual world. The expression, ' Cosmic Word,' which goes through all times and all peoples, expresses an absolutely true fact of the Spirit-Land.

In our present age we can only understand what is meant by the Cosmic Word if we approach the peculiarities of the spiritual world in the way we have endeavoured to describe in this lecture. As in the spiritual teachings of the various ages and peoples, more or less comprehensible allusion has been made to the Cosmic Word, so in this age of ours, in order that mankind may not be devastated by materialism, it is necessary that man should acquire an understanding for such words as those spoken in reference to the Spirit-Land. ' In this place words are deeds, and other deeds must follow these.' It is necessary for our age, that when such words are spoken from the knowledge of the spiritual world, souls should feel their reality, should feel that they do represent reality. We must know in how far this is just as much a characteristic of the spiritual world as when we employ the ordinary sense-ideas in order to characterise the the physical sense-world.

As to how far our present age brings understanding to bear on such words as : ' Here in this place words are deeds, and other deeds must follow these,' thereon will depend the understanding with which it receives Spiritual Science, and the right preparation by the men of to-day to guard against the entrance of that materialism which must otherwise dominate and bring the civilisation of humanity ever more and more into a state of impoverishment, devastation and decline.

LECTURE 5

Munich, 28th August, 1913.

I should like to do all that is possible to bring about a good understanding of the conditions in the spiritual realms with which we wish to become acquainted in the course of these lectures. For this reason I should like to introduce, as a little episode at the beginning of what we are about to consider this evening, a story calculated to clear up for us many a question which we have already considered and shall still have to consider.

At a certain time ' Professor Capesius ' was much disturbed and puzzled in his mind ; the reason for this was as follows. *The Portal of Initiation* will have shown you that Capesius was a professor of history—an historian. Now occult research has revealed to me the fact that a number of well-known modern historians whom I could name, have become such because they were in some way connected with the Egyptian Initiation, in the Third Post-Atlantean age of civilisation. They were either directly concerned with Initiation, or in some way or other they had approached the Mysteries of the Temple. You will have noted that Capesius was an historian who did not depend merely upon external documents, but also tried to arrive at the ideas which play a part in history—either in the evolution of humanity, or in the unfolding of civilisations.

I must admit that whilst trying to draw the character of Capesius in *The Portal of Initiation*, in *The Soul's Probation*, and in *The Guardian of the Threshold*, I always had before me his relation to the Egyptian Initiation-principle, which is expressed in closer detail in *The Soul's Awakening* in scenes seven and eight. It should be borne firmly in mind that the experiences which the soul of Capesius passed through during his Egyptian incarnation form the basis of all the later strokes of destiny which overtook this soul, and they must be taken into account at the present time. As a professor of history, Capesius in his professorial life concerned himself chiefly with all that has developed through the growth and existence of peoples, of civilisations, and of individual persons, in the successive epochs of evolution.

One day, however, Capesius came across some of the literature of Haeckel. He then made himself acquainted with this entire conception of the universe (a subject with which he had previously occupied himself but little), and in connection therewith he read all kinds of writings about the world being made of atoms. That was the reason for his feeling so miserable, and the frame of mind that overcame him was a peculiar one when, at a comparatively late period of life, he became acquainted with this atomistic Haeckelism. His reason said : ' One really cannot come to a correct understanding of the world around one if one refuses to explain the phenomena of nature by atoms—through a mechanical conception of the universe.' In other words, Capesius came to see more and more what is, in a certain sense, and from one aspect, correct in atomism, the mechanical view of nature. He was not one of those who fanatically reject such a thing as a matter of course ; for he had confidence in his reason, and much in this way of looking at things seemed to him necessary for the understanding of the phenomena of surrounding nature. Yet this troubled him, for he said to himself : ' How desolate, how unsatisfying for the human soul is this conception of nature ! How badly fares every idea one wants to gain concerning spirit and spirit-beings, and about what belongs to the soul.'

Thus Capesius found himself swept backwards and forwards by doubts, and he set forth—I might almost say, instinctively—along the path that he had often taken when things weighed heavily on his soul ; he went to the cottage of Felix Balde to hold converse with those good people, a talk with whom had often rendered his soul such good, true service. Ofttimes had Capesius been refreshed by what Felicia Balde could give him in her wonderful fairy-tales. And so he went to them. At first, as Dame Felicia was busy in the house when he arrived, he met only with Felix Balde, the Father Felix of whom he had grown so fond as time went on. To him he confided his troubles, the doubts which had laid hold upon him through having become acquainted with Haeckel and the theory of atoms. He first of all explained to him how necessary it appeared to his reason to apply something of this sort to the phenomena of nature, and on the other hand, he showed good Father Felix how barren and unsatisfying is such a conception of the universe. Capesius was greatly perturbed when he went to Father Felix seeking, so to speak, help for his soul.

Now Father Felix was of different nature from Capesius ; he went his own special way ; he put from him at once anything like Haeckelism and the atomistic theory of the universe by explaining to our good Professor Capesius how the matter really stood. He said to him : ' Certainly there must be atoms ; it is quite correct to talk of atoms ; but we must clearly understand that these atoms, if in some way they are to form the world, must so arrange themselves and settle with regard to each other, that this arrangement corresponds to the laws of measure and number, that the atom of the one substance is composed of a totality of four, another of three, another of two, another of one ; in this way the substances that are in the world came into being.' It seemed to Capesius, who was well informed in history, that this was somewhat Pythagorean ; he felt that the Pythagorean principle was dominant in Felix Balde. Felix Balde wanted to make it clear to him that one can make nothing of the atoms themselves, but that within these there are the wise laws of measure and number ; and ever more and more complicated became what Father Felix explained in ever increasingly complicated numerical relations, in accordance with which Cosmic Wisdom groups the atoms together, and asserts itself among the atoms as a spiritual principle. More and more complicated became the figures that Father Felix built up for Capesius. Then Capesius was overcome by a strange feeling, a mood such as might be described by saying that he had so to exert himself to combine all this complicated stuff, that—in spite of the fact that the subject interested him very much—he had to suppress a kind of yawning, and he fell almost into a kind of dreamy state.

But before our good Capesius had completely fallen into a dream-state, Balde's wife arrived, and first of all she, too, had to listen for a while to the whole explanation of numbers and figures. She sat patiently down. She had a peculiar way with her, namely, when she was not quite in sympathy with anything—sympathetic in a good sense—and felt it necessary to control a feeling of boredom, she clasped her hands together and twirled her thumbs, and when she did that she could always entirely repress her yawns. After she had done this for a little while there came a pause, and she could now try to wake Capesius up again by means of a refreshing story. And here Felicia related to the good professor the following story.

Once upon a time, in a very lonely region stood a great castle. In this great castle lived many people, old and young, and they were all more or less related to one another and belonged to one another in some sort of way.

These people formed a self-contained community. They were, in a sense, shut off from the rest of the world ; for round about, far and wide, neither men nor human settlements were to be found, and in time this state of things proved a great distress for many of these people ; as a result many of them became visionary ; they had visions which might well indeed, from the manner in which they made their appearance, have related to something real. Felicia then told how a great number of these people had similar visions. First they had the vision of a great figure of light which came down from the clouds ; a

60

figure of light which, when it came down, brought warmth with it as it sank into the hearts and souls of the inhabitants of the castle. And, so ran Felicia's story, it was really felt that something illuminating had come down from the heights of heaven, through this figure of light which came from above.

But soon—so the story continued—all those who had the vision of this figure of light saw something more. They saw how from all sides, from all around the mountain, as though scrambling out of the earth, there came all kinds of blackish-brown, steel-grey forms. Whereas the figure of light coming from above was a single one, many, very many of these other forms, came round about the castle. Whereas the figure of light entered more into the hearts, more into the souls, these other beings—one might call them elementary beings —were like besiegers of the castle.

So for a long time the people in the castle—and there was a fair number of them—lived between that which came from above and that which laid siege to the castle. One day, however, it appeared that the form from above sank down lower than heretofore, and also that the besiegers were coming further in. An uncomfortable feeling spread among the visionaries in the castle— we must bear in mind that Felicia was narrating a fairy-tale—and these visionaries, together with the other inhabitants of the castle, passed into a dream-like condition. The figure from above divided into separate clouds of light, but these were seized upon by the besiegers of the castle and were darkened by them. The result of this was that gradually the inhabitants of the castle fell into a dream-condition, and the earth-life of the inhabitants of the castle was thereby prolonged for centuries. After some hundreds of years they came to themselves ; but found themselves divided into small communities and settled in many different parts of the earth. Also they inhabited smaller castles, which were like copies of the great castle they had inhabited centuries before ; and it was seen that what they had experienced in the old castle was now in their souls as psychic strength, psychic possessions, psychic health. From these castles they could well carry on all sorts of employments, such as agriculture, stock-farming, and the like. They became hard-working people, good agriculturists, healthy both in soul and body.

When Felicia had told all this, good Professor Capesius was, as ever, pleasantly affected by her story. But her husband, Father Felix, felt it necessary to add something to it by way of explanation of this tale, which she had not been told before. So he said : 'The figure which came from above out of the clouds was that of the Luciferic Principle, and the forms that came from outside like besiegers, they were the Ahrimanic Principle, and so on,' and Father Felix's explanations became more and more complicated. At first Felicia

61

listened, then folded her hands together and twiddled her thumbs ; but at last she said, as Father Felix was becoming more and more complicated : ' Well, I must now go into the kitchen and look after things, for we have potato-rissoles to-day, and they will be too much cooked.' . . . So she slipped away into the kitchen. The effect produced upon Capesius by good Father Felix's explanations was such that he could no longer listen to him and although he was very fond of Father Felix he really no longer heard correctly what the latter was saying by way of explanation.

Here I must add the remark that what I have just related happened to Capesius at a time when he was already acquainted with Benedictus. In fact he was, as we might say, a good pupil of his and he had often heard Benedictus explain the relationship between the Luciferic and the Ahrimanic elements. Although Capesius was a very clever man, he was never really able to understand the explanations of Benedictus concerning the Luciferic and Ahrimanic elements. There was always something wanting ; and he could not make head or tail of it all. So this time he went his way turning over in his mind this story of the castle that multiplied itself. Then he came once more to Benedictus, and, behold, Benedictus could perceive that something had taken place in the soul of Capesius. Capesius himself had noticed that every time he recalled the story of the castle that multiplied itself, his soul was peculiarly stirred within him. It seemed as if this story worked upon his soul, developing strength within it, as though his soul became strengthened by it. Consequently he was always repeating it to himself, as if in meditation. And now he came again to Benedictus, who noticed that the forces of Capesius' soul had been strengthened within him. So Benedictus explained the following to him in a peculiar manner, and whereas formerly Professor Capesius would, perhaps, on account of his learning, have understood less well the explanations of Benedictus, he now understood them extremely well. What had fallen into his soul through Felicia's story was like a seed which fructified the forces of his soul.

Benedictus said : ' Let us now consider three things ! First of all we shall consider human thought, human concepts, the thoughts that a man can carry about within him, through which he makes the world comprehensible to himself whenever he is alone. To have thoughts and inwardly explain things in complete solitude, that a man can do entirely for himself. For that he is not compelled to attach himself to anyone else. In fact, he can think things out best when he shuts himself up in his study and, in quiet self-contained thought, with the full strength of his thinking-power, tries to understand the world and its phenomena. ' Now,' said Benedictus, ' when a man thus proceeds with his thoughts, it always happens to the individual that the feeling element in the soul works up into his thoughts and concepts.   Thereby there comes always to man the temptation, the attraction, of the Luciferic element.   It is inconceivable for a man to ruminate and reason, and philosophise and give himself explanations about the things in the world, without there coming into his thought an impulse from his feeling soul, and thereby a Luciferic element comes into his solitary thinking.   Thoughts formed by an individual person are always permeated, in great part, grasped and permeated by the Luciferic element.' Whereas formerly Capesius had understood but little when Benedictus had spoken of the Luciferic and Ahrimanic elements, it was now a matter of course for him to understand that in the solitary thoughts that a man forms within himself there must lurk the allurements of the Luciferic element.   He now understood that in the activity of a person sunk in solitary thought Lucifer has always a point of vantage, from which he can snatch that man out of the progressive path of the world's evolution, and—since the person detaches himself from the world in his solitary thought—from which he can lead him to the lonely island separated from the rest of the cosmic order, which Lucifer wants to set up, with the object of establishing there all that has a tendency to separate itself.

Thus Benedictus first of all directed Capesius' attention to solitary, personal, inner thought.   'And now,' said he, 'we shall turn our attention to something else.   We shall consider what we meet with in writing.   In writing we have a remarkable element of human civilisation.   When we consider the significance of thought, we must say : Thought, in the first place, lives in the individual man.   It is accessible to Lucifer, because Lucifer wants to lead what belongs to the soul away from the physical world and isolate it.   But this solitary thinking is not accessible to Ahriman ; for it is subject to the normal laws of the coming into being and passing away of the physical plane.   Writing is different ; for by being put into writing, thought is snatched from destruction —it is made permanent.'

Now, I have directed your attention to the fact that Ahriman's continual endeavour is to rescue from the stream of destruction that which lives in human thought, and to retain it in the physical world.   That is the characteristic process which causes one to write things.   Human thought, which would otherwise pass away in time, is thus fixed, and preserved for all time.   Precisely here does Ahriman enter into human civilisation.   Although Capesius was no reactionary, and did not hold with those who want to do away with writing or forbid it in the state-schools, he understood that as man is everywhere piling up books upon books, the Ahrimanic impulse has entered the evolution of civilisation.   Now he knew that in solitary thought there is the Luciferic attraction ; and in writing, in all that becomes fixed through writing or printing, there is the Ahrimanic element ! He knew that even in the external world, human evolution cannot exist without Ahrimanic and Luciferic elements being at work everywhere. And he now understood that for the very reason that with the progress of civilisation writing becomes of more and more importance (and to recognise this one need not be clairvoyant, but need only trace back evolution for a few centuries), he knew that because of this the Ahrimanic element must also gain more and more in importance as civilisation progresses. And to-day, when it has become of such great significance—this was quite clear to Capesius—we have great Ahrimanic citadels. It is not yet customary— Spiritual Science has not yet brought things so far—for the truth to be so far openly spoken in public life that when a student is going to a library he says : ' I am now going to browse in Ahriman's citadel ! ' nevertheless, it would be the truth. Libraries, great and small, are the citadels of Ahriman, they are the strongholds from which he can exercise the greatest influence upon the evolution of human civilisation. In such respects one must look facts straight in the face.

Benedictus then explained to Capesius something further. He said to him : ' Well and good ; on the one side we have the thoughts in the individual human being which belong to Lucifer, on the other we have the written works which belong to Ahriman ; but between the two we have a middle condition. In what is Luciferic we have a united whole ; man strives after unity when he wants to explain the world to himself in thought, but in what is written—in writing—we have something that is atomistic.' Then Benedictus showed Capesius something that again he could quite well follow, in consequence of the refreshing of his mind through the story told by Dame Felicia. He explained that between solitary thought and writing we have the word—the word, with which we cannot be alone as with our thoughts. Through the word we live in a community. We can think alone, in isolation. There is a purpose in thinking alone ; but a person would not use words if he wished to go alone. Speech has its significance in intercourse.

Thus the word is brought out of the solitude of the human personality, and unfolds itself in communion with others. The word is the embodied thought, but at the same time for the physical plane it is something quite different from thought. We need not enter into the clairvoyant results to which in various lectures I have drawn attention, but external history shows us,—and, being an historian, Capesius understood this very well,—even by means of external history we can see that the word or speech must originally have had quite a different relation to mankind from that which obtains at the present time. As we go further and further back in the various languages, we perceive that we must eventually come—as occult observation shows—to an original human language which embraced the whole globe, and which has only gradually become differentiated. Even if we go back to the Hebrew,—and in this respect the Hebrew language is specially remarkable,—in the Hebrew words we find something different from what is found in the words of Western Europe. In Hebrew the words are much less conventional; they have a soul, so to speak, so that one feels the sense in them; they express more of their necessary meaning. The further we go back in evolution the more we find languages similar to the original common language. What is narrated of the Tower of Babel is symbolic of the fact that there really was one primeval language originally, and that this became differentiated into the different languages of peoples and tribes. Owing to the fact that that common primeval language became differentiated into the languages of peoples and tribes, the word has, as it were, come half-way towards the solitude of thought. Every individual does not use a language of his own,—if that were so, language would have no meaning,—but groups of people speak a common tongue. Thus the word has become a middle thing between solitary thought and the primeval language.

In the primeval language a word was understood through its sound, through that which was its sound-value; it was not necessary to get more conventional information about the value of the sound; for in the primeval language was found the soul of the word. That has, as we have said, now become differentiated. Whatever brings about separation works also into the hands of Lucifer, so that human beings, when they formed differentiated languages, received thereby a principle of separation, that is, they entered into the current which makes it easy for Lucifer to lift men out of the general order of the world which had already been arranged before Lucifer was there; it thus became easy to set man upon an isolated island, to separate him from the rest of the progressive path of the evolution of humanity. Thus, in the element of speech, of the word, there lies a middle condition. If the word had been what it ought to have become, if the Luciferic influence had not pounced upon the word, then the word would have represented that middle divine condition;—free from Lucifer and Ahriman,—in which man can move in complete harmony with the progressive divine spiritual order of the cosmos. Thus, the word was influenced on the one side Luciferically. Whereas thought when formed in solitude, is almost entirely under the Luciferic element, the word, on the other hand, as I have explained, is laid hold of by the Luciferic element from the one side.

But on the other side also, writing reacts upon the word, and the further humanity progresses the greater significance does writing acquire for language. This is because the dialects which have had nothing to do with writing are gradually sinking into the background, and what is even called the language of literature frequently appears as the more elegant element. That indicates that language is reacted upon by writing. In certain parts this can be seen very clearly. I always recall something that I noticed in my school-mates and myself. In Austria, where there is such a mixture of dialects, great importance is attached in the schools to the pupils learning a literary language which, for the most part, they had not spoken before. The acquiring of this literary language had a special effect. I can speak quite impartially about this because I myself was exposed to the peculiar effect of this literary language, Austrian school-German, for a long time, and have only with difficulty lost the habit of it ;—even yet it sometimes makes its appearance. The peculiarity consists in this, that all the short vowels are pronounced long, and all the long ones short ; whereas the dialect, the language which is born from the word, pronounces them correctly. When, for example, one means the sun that is in the sky (' Sonne '), the dialect says ' d'Sunn ; ' but when one has gone to the Austrian schools one is tempted to say ' die Soone.' The dialect says ' Sun ' for ' Sohn ; ' the Austrian school-tongue gives ' Sonn.' Thus one says ' die Soone ' and ' der Sonn.' Naturally that is an extreme case, but it clings to one, or at least it did cling.

There one sees how writing reacts upon language. But it does generally react. We only need set the progress of civilisation clearly before our mind ; we then see how, precisely with the progress of civilisation, the language loses what is vital, elementary and organic, what has grown on the soil, and people come to speak more and more a book-language. Here we have from the other side what is Ahrimanic—the reaction upon the word of that which is always in literature. He who wants to evolve in accordance with nature will, in this very example of the three things which Benedictus chose for Capesius, see how senseless it would be to wish to eliminate Ahriman and Lucifer from evolution. As Benedictus shows, three things come into consideration : the solitary thought, the word, and the script.

Now no one who thinks soundly, even if he has quite understood the truth that Lucifer's influence must underlie all solitary thought, and Ahriman's influence must underlie script, no one will want to root out Lucifer's influence where it is so obviously at work ; for that would mean to forbid solitary thought. It must be admitted that many would consider that a most comfortable arrangement ; but no one would like openly to advocate it. On the other hand we should not want to do away with writing; what we must do is to admit that just as positive and negative electricity indicate a contrast in external physical nature, so the Ahrimanic and the Luciferic must form a contrast which must be there. They are two poles, neither of which can be omitted, but they must be brought into relation according to measure and number : then man can move between them both in that middle line by way of the word. It is the mission of the word to contain wisdom, knowledge, thoughts, concepts ; for example, a man can say to himself : I must so develop myself within the word that through the word I allow all that is capricious, all that is personal, to be corrected in me by the word, by receiving into my soul that which has been brought forth in the word, the word filled with the wisdom of all ages. Attention must be given not only to one's own opinion, not only to what one thinks oneself and can recognise as correct through one's own powers, but respect must be felt for that which has resulted through the civilisations and the efforts in wisdom made by the different races in the course of historical development. That signifies the bringing of Lucifer on the one side, so to speak, into the correct relation to the word. We must not do away with isolated thinking, but must note that the word belongs to intercourse and we must trace up the word through the ages ; the more we do this the more we give Lucifer the right influence over the word. We do not then succumb to the authority of the word, rather do we protect the word that carries the wisdom of the earth from one epoch of civilisation to another. On the other hand, it is the duty of the man who perceives correctly how the matter stands, not to succumb to the rigid, authoritative principle that lies in writing ; for, whether it contains the holiest or the most profane, man thereby falls a victim to Ahriman. We must clearly understand that for external material civilisation man had to have writing, but that writing is something whereby Ahriman, for this indeed is his task, wants to detach thought from the current of destruction. He does not want to let it flow into the stream of death. Hence, in writing, we have the best means of keeping thought upon the physical plane. We must confront in full consciousness the fact that in what is written we have the Ahrimanic element; we never allow writing to gain the upper hand over mankind ; in short, we must keep the Word in the middle position, so that, as it were, from right and left, from thinking and from writing, there work the two polar opposites, Lucifer and Ahriman. If we clearly realise that there must always be opposites, we shall be taking up the right position.

When Capesius had heard this, and had received it with his soul-forces which had been strengthened by Felicia, his attitude to what Benedictus could now explain to him was quite different from his former one when Benedictus had also explained to him the Luciferic and Ahrimanic elements. Through the fact that the fairy-tales which fertilised the forces of his soul, inspired as they were from the spiritual world, influenced him more and more—through this Capesius himself gained the experience that the capacities and powers of his soul were inwardly strengthened. That is represented in the thirteenth scene of *The Soul's Awakening* where the one soul-force in Capesius, represented as Philia, meets him really tangibly in the spirit and not merely as an abstract force in his soul. In the same measure in which Philia grew to an entity within the soul of Capesius, did he understand more and more what Benedictus really wanted from him. At the time when he heard the specially fruitful story about the castle which multiplied itself—which developed into a number—it did not at once work in him, he almost fell asleep and especially had he almost fallen asleep when Father Felix was talking about the atoms. But now this soul of Capesius, after having thus matured, recognised that there is a triad in the whole stream of the world's evolution—on the one side, the Luciferic, solitary thought ; on the other the Ahrimanic, writing ; the third, the middle condition, the purely Divine. He now recognised the number three in this most significant factor of the evolution of civilisation on the physical plane, and he could surmise that this number three is to be sought for everywhere. The attitude of Capesius to the law of numbers now became different : now through the awakening of Philia in him, he felt the nature of number in the development of the world ; and now the nature of measure became also clear to him. He saw that in every triad there are two that stand as opposites to each other and these must be set in harmony in mutual moderation. Capesius recognised a mighty cosmic law, concerning which he now knew that it must exist in some way or other not only on the physical plane, but also in the higher worlds. We shall have to speak further about this in the more subtle elucidations of the divine spiritual world. He divined that he had penetrated to a law which exists on the physical plane as though covered with a veil, and that, possessing this knowledge, he had something wherewith he could cross the Threshold ; and when he crosses the Threshold he then enters the spiritual world and must leave behind him all that is aroused merely through physical experience.

Number and Measure—he had learned to feel them, to feel them deeply, to experience them ; and now he also understood when Benedictus brought up other things, in the first place still simple ones, in order to bring the principle more fully before him. For instance, Benedictus said to Capesius : ' The same domination of the triad, of polarity or opposition in the triad, of harmonious balance, can be found at other points of existence. One might, for instance, consider something from another point of view, *viz.*, thinking, inner imagination. The inner concept of things, the working out within oneself of the cosmic secrets—that is one thing ; the second is pure perception, let us say, simple listening. There are people who are naturally more prone to reflect upon things introspectively ; again there are others who do not care to think, who always listen, receive everything by listening, take everything on authority, even when it is the authority of natural phenomena ; for there is also the dogma of external experience ; that is, if one lets oneself be imposed upon by natural phenomena. Now Benedictus could easily show Professor Capesius that in solitary thought there again lies the Luciferic attraction ; and in mere listening, mere perceiving, the Ahrimanic element. But one may keep the middle path and go, as it were, between the two. It is not necessary to stay at abstract introspective thinking, whereby one shuts oneself up like a hermit within one's soul, nor to give oneself up to mere listening and attending to that which can be observed by the eyes and ears. One can do yet another thing, by making what one thinks so alive within one, so forceful, that one's own thoughts appear before one as living things and one may immerse oneself in them as into something that one hears and sees externally, so that one's own thought becomes as concrete as that which one sees and hears. That is a middle condition. In the mere thinking which is the foundation of brooding, Lucifer approaches a man ; in mere listening or attending, be it through perceiving or through the authority of men, there lies the Ahrimanic element. When a man inwardly arouses and strengthens his soul so that he sees or hears his thoughts, as it were, he has arrived at meditation. Meditation is a middle condition. It is neither thinking nor perceiving ; it is a thinking that is as alive in the soul as perception and it is a perception that externally has nothing but thoughts as its object. Between the Luciferic element of thinking and the Ahrimanic element of perceiving, the life of the soul flows on in meditation, as in the Divine-Spiritual element that alone bears within it the progress of the cosmic phenomena. The man who meditates—who so lives in his thoughts that they become as alive within him as are perceptions in him—lives in the Divine onflowing stream. On his right hand he has the mere thoughts and on his left the merely Ahrimanic element, the mere listening ; and he shuts out neither the one nor the other, for he knows that he lives in a triad, that number rules life ; and he knows that there is a polarity, a contrast, an opposition between which meditation flows along. And he knows that, each in its proper measure, the Luciferic and the Ahrimanic elements must keep the balance in meditation.

In all the different domains man learns this cosmic principle of number and measure which Capesius, after his soul had been prepared, learned through the instruction of Benedictus. Thus, the soul which wants to prepare itself for the knowledge of the spiritual world gradually accustoms itself to seek in the world, at every point that can be reached, for number, and, above all, for the number three ; so that it sees the polar opposites through which everything must reveal itself and the necessity for these opposites to balance each other. A middle condition cannot be a mere streaming on, but everywhere we must so experience the stream that we must direct the vision of our soul to the right and the left and steer our vessel as the third between the right and left polar opposites. Feeling this, Capesius learned through Benedictus how to steer aright into the spiritual worlds—to cross the Threshold of the Spiritual World. And each person who wants to penetrate into Spiritual Science will have to learn this, that he may attain to a true understanding of the real knowledge of the higher worlds.

LECTURE 6

Munich, 29th August, 1913.

There are still a few more remarks to be made in connection with what was said in the preceding lecture. For we have seen that in order to enter the domain of Spirit with clairvoyant consciousness, and to cross the Threshold of the Spiritual World as one should, it is necessary to leave behind us all the perceptions of the physical world and also all that can be undertaken in the physical world with the ordinary thinking, feeling and willing; we must be prepared to stand before phenomena and beings having characteristics that have nothing in common with what can be observed and experienced in the world of the senses. For this it first is necessary to strengthen the faculties of the soul. These faculties, these strengthened, fortified faculties of the soul must be carried up; we must bring something with us when we cross the Threshold into the domain of Spirit. We have drawn attention to the fact that everything the sense-world can give us, the ideas and feelings which we acquire within the sense-world, are all images of what is perceptible to the senses. Nothing that we acquire in this way can be of use in the spiritual world; but whatever is not a picture of the sense-world and has no significance at first for that world— although it can be evoked within it and developed in a free inner soul-life— that must be carried up into the supersensible worlds. Thus, it has been pointed out how one may acquire concepts of the triad as a numerical relationship, a measured co-operation of opposites (in which we specially noted the Luciferic and Ahrimanic elements) and a middle condition. Such ideas have not in the first place a direct significance in the physical world. Obviously one can get along in the physical world without these, but one must have formed them for oneself in this world if one wants to carry them up into the spiritual worlds.

Because of this I endeavoured by means of the teachings of Benedictus to direct attention to the fact of how, in the development of human civilisation on the physical plane, in the triad of thought, word and script, there works something Luciferic and something Ahrimanic, as well as the middle condition.

In connection with this I shall only just remark that here many things come into consideration which, if we get the right perspective, can really be of the greatest use for the understanding of human life and which man must acquire from the present time onwards if civilisation is to progress aright. It will be recognised that soon we shall no longer be satisfied with the concepts we now form for ourselves, based on the conditions from which the easy-going humanity of the day likes to form its ideas concerning the various ages and peoples. We have among the civilised European nations those who speak different languages and those who differ as regards their written characters. The Western peoples of Europe use the so-called Roman characters in writing—these letters are used in various languages—but there are other European nations using quite different forms of letters. In Europe we have the fact that besides the Roman letters there are also the so-called Gothic, and that these exist side by side. That is a significant phenomenon when we want to review the civilisation of Europe.

Such things are apparently small symptoms, but these symptoms point to very deep foundations of existence. Nations which employ different written characters will only attain a correct reciprocal understanding when they take into consideration that this understanding must be brought about through the mutual comprehension of a spiritual element. For nations that use different characters in writing (thereby giving a special foothold to the Ahrimanic impulse) it does not suffice to have an understanding merely according to the requirements of the physical plane, but the spiritual element must be understood by both nations, and in this harmony must be sought. For nations that use written characters such as the Roman, it is necessary, in order to understand one another, that they should carry the spiritual element so far as to begin to have a mutual understanding of one another as regards also the things of the physical plane. One who understands such things as have just been mentioned can recognise this, in regard to the reciprocal relations of the national life of Europe. It is of deep significance that in Central Europe, in order, as it were, to express the peculiar relationship of the Ahrimanic and Luciferic elements, the two kinds of writing are employed side by side. The reason for this is that here a middle condition can only be reached under special difficulties, so that the Roman alphabet which is more exposed to the Ahrimanic element, must be brought into a certain opposition to the Gothic, which is more exposed to the Luciferic element ; and it is characteristic that in their handwriting many people have to mingle the Gothic and the Roman scripts. Such an intermingling is of immense significance, pointing, as it does, to something that lies deep in the substrata of the soul, for it points to the significant fact of the special manner in which such people have to arrange their relations with the Luciferic and Ahrimanic elements. Hence it comes about that many a person has to make great efforts, in writing German, not to fall into the Gothic writing when he wants to write in Roman style, and not to fall into the Roman when he wants to use German letters. It will become more and more necessary to observe life in such minute details and to observe the symptoms which bring to the surface what is taking place in the hidden depths. By such means we shall learn to acquire in the physical world ideas, feelings and concepts such as we can with advantage carry across the Threshold into the realm of the spirit.

One must certainly be awake to the fact that the civilisation of our day has an absolute genius for superficiality regarding anything which in any way expresses the spirit. Thus even in the physical world we must acquire some idea of that which shines out of the spiritual world and sends its rays into the physical sense-world. Let us therefore see how, in one other realm, the Luciferic and Ahrimanic elements play into the physical world. Let us speak first of the realm of art. Here it may absolutely be maintained that what has already been stated is correct, namely, that the Luciferic impulse plays a part in all artistic development of humanity ; that the Luciferic element, as I have shown, is present to a very great extent in the art-development of humanity. But there is something more. When we consider the arts and how we meet with them in the physical world, we have in the first place five principal ones : the art of building or architecture, sculpture, painting, music and poetry. There are certain arts which mingle with various elements in the arts just mentioned— mingle or connect them with one another, for example, the art of dancing, which combines several. When one rightly understands that art, one does so from what is fundamental in the various arts. Naturally, these can be also combined quite differently. Of the five arts those of architecture and of sculpture are especially exposed to the Ahrimanic impulse ; the Ahrimanic impulses enter into architecture and sculpture. Here we have to do with forms. To accomplish anything in architecture or sculpture, we must enter into the element of form. This element of form is principally dominant on the physical plane. Here the real rulers are the Spirits of Form. We must dive down into their spiritual element if we want to make ourselves acquainted with them, as I said when speaking figuratively of putting one's head into an ant-heap. Every-one who has anything to do with the element of sculpture must plunge his head into the living element of the Spirits of Form. Now in the realm of the physical world, the Spirits of Form act conjointly with the Ahrimanic element.

Especially in such a case as this we see how necessary it is not simply to say in an externally superficial manner that we must protect ourselves from the

Ahrimanic element; for we must always take into account that such beings as the Ahrimanic and the Luciferic have their appointed domain in which, normally they have to live and work, and that bad effects come about only when they overstep their boundaries. The Ahrimanic impulses have their absolutely legitimate domain in architecture and sculpture.

If, on the other hand, we take the musical and poetic elements, here we have arts wherein, in a more restricted sense, the Luciferic impulses are at work. In a certain sense we may say that poetry and music are the arts influenced by Lucifer and architecture and sculpture those influenced by Ahriman. As in a certain sense thought runs its course in the solitude of the soul and thereby separates itself from united activity, even so have the experiences of poetry and music something that belongs to the inner part of the soul where they directly encounter the Luciferic impulse. Even if in the arts of building and architecture we must observe national limitations—for wherever Ahriman is, there, too, does Lucifer play his part—even if to a certain degree these arts are modified according to the character of the people, we may say, nevertheless, that this element remains in a certain sense neutral. Poetry is essentially connected with that Luciferic element which finds its expression in the differences of national character. In music we do not notice it much, but there is also something that leads to differentiation, more than is the case in architecture and sculpture.

Just in such a domain as this we see again that in the forming of concepts for the higher worlds we cannot get on in such a comfortable fashion as many would like to do. It is absolutely correct to say that the Ahrimanic element works more in architecture and sculpture, and the Luciferic more in poetry and music; yet it must be said that so soon as one has to do with concepts which are also valid in the higher worlds, the task is not so easy that one can simply answer at once when asked, 'Does Ahriman or Lucifer work more in architecture?' Certainly on the physical plane it is easy to give correct information when asked, 'What colour is the common chicory?' We answer that it is blue. People would like things to be just as easy as regards the higher worlds; but it is wrong to suppose that one can obtain such easy answers there. Still, although what I have just said holds good, the following is absolutely true: With regard to architecture it is generally the case that the Ahrimanic element exercises the strongest impulse; in sculpture, however, the opposing Luciferic impulses may be so strong that there can be plastic works in which Lucifer is more dominant than Ahriman. Nevertheless, what was said before is correct; for in the spiritual world there is not only the faculty of transformation, but one may say: everything is everywhere. Each spiritual element tries, in reality, to permeate everything. There can be Luciferic sculpture despite the

74

truth that the Ahrimanic influence is predominant in sculpture. We must, therefore, say that whereas poetry is chiefly under the influence of Lucifer, the Ahrimanic influence can work to a high degree on music ; so that there can be music in which there is much more that is Ahrimanic than Luciferic, although it is true that music is primarily subject to the influence of Lucifer.

In the middle line, between what is Ahrimanic in architecture and plastic art and what is Luciferic in poetry and music, there lies painting ; this is a neutral domain, so to speak, but not such that one can settle down comfortably in it and say : ' Now I will just work at my painting, for neither Ahriman nor Lucifer can trouble me in that ! ' In painting we must remember that just in this middle line we are most of all exposed to the Luciferic and Ahrimanic attacks from both sides and that at every moment we have to be on our guard ; for in the realm of painting we are most thoroughly exposed to the one or the other influence. The middle line is always the one wherein, in the very strictest sense of the word, we have to bring about by means of the human will and human act, an harmonious agreement between the polarities, between the opposites.

Thus we see, when we consider these domains, as we have just done—it could be done just as well in others—we acquire certain concepts, without which we can assuredly get along on the physical plane. For it is obvious that if a person wants to remain superficial and shallow, he can get along on the physical plane, even if he does not consider music Luciferic and architecture Ahrimanic. But if he wants to manage without these ideas, then on the physical plane he cannot form any concepts, ideas and feelings adapted so to strengthen the soul that it may cross the Threshold in a favourable manner and rise into the realm of Spirit ; he will have to remain here below, on the physical plane.

Thus, if we really want to cross the Threshold, we must acquire concepts, feelings and ideas for the realm of Spirit which are indeed evoked by the physical but which pass beyond the physical sense-region. If, having thus strengthened the soul, we cross the Threshold of the Spiritual world, we become familiar with a world in which takes place what we have described as the spiritual converse of living thought-beings, which so reveals itself that within it beings are present which consist solely of thought-substance, yet indeed so that they are far more real, personal and individual, than the human beings on the earth. As a man in his flesh and blood is a real being on the physical plane, so are they real in their thought-substance. We become at home in that world, wherein a thought-language passes between one being and another, and where the soul is obliged to carry on thought-conversations if it is to come into relation with the thought-beings who live in these worlds. I have intimated this in the book, *The Threshold of the Spiritual World*. Here many a supplementary detail can be added. With all the responsibility with which a thing of that sort should be carried out, I have endeavoured to avoid, in this book, a systematic presentation, but rather to say certain things in an aphoristic form that can be useful even if one has already absorbed all that has been said in former books and cycles.

As a living thought-being, one must familiarise oneself with the realm of Spirit of which one can say : 'Here in this place words are deeds, and other deeds must follow these.' Whereas in the physcial world we accomplish our deeds as man through the movement of our hand,—thoughts, which live in the Cosmic World in the sense described, are direct acts. What is spoken, is done. That is the point as regards the spiritual world. In the language of spirit what one being does to another is at the same time that which he does to the external spirit-world lying around him. What is said is everywhere an act. Thus we must raise our life into the realm of spirit and there we find ourselves as living thought-beings among other living thought-beings. We must behave as do the other living beings, that is, let our words be acts,—if one may use such simple words.

What do we find there ? For our own self we no longer find that which we have in the physical or even in the elementary world. This self that we carry through the physical and elementary worlds is a sum-total of experiences gathered from the impressions of the physical world and from what arises from the thinking, feeling and willing which the soul develops on the physical plane. But neither the impressions, nor thinking, nor feeling, nor willing, have any significance at all for the spiritual world, in the form in which they meet us on the physical plane. Consequently, in the spiritual world, we find something else instead of the so-called human self of the physical plane and of the elementary world ; we find that part of oneself which is, indeed, always present in the depths of the soul, but of which the ordinary consciousness of the physical plane has no knowledge ; we find our other self there, as a second being. We find our other self in the spiritual world.

At the close of these lectures I shall draw attention, as I have done in the closing chapter of the book, *The Threshold of the Spiritual World* (for those who would like to point out contradictions), to the manner in which the terms employed here are related to those I have used as terminology in my *Theosophy* and *Occult Science*. But here it may be said, that a man lives in his physical body in the physical world around him. When he leaves it, when he has experiences outside his physical body, he experiences in his etheric body, and has as environment the elementary world ; and when he comes out of that, too, he then experiences the Spirit-land in his astral body. With this experience—this feeling oneself in the astral body—there comes about another meeting, which one has in the spiritual world ; the meeting with the other self, that second self of which Johannes Thomasius speaks at the end of *The Guardian of the Threshold*, and which, throughout the whole course of *The Soul's Awakening* stands by the side of the first self, as it were, beside Johannes Thomasius, and calls forth the experiences. We must comment further on the principal part played by this other self ; it is that which a man learns to know when he learns to feel, to perceive, to experience in the spiritual world in his astral body ; this it is which goes from earth-life to earth-life, from incarnation to incarnation. This which thus goes from earth-life to earth-life, interweaves itself so mysteriously into the nature of a human being during one earth-life between birth and death, that the physical consciousness cannot as a rule perceive this other self ; for it is in the spiritual world, although it is at the same time bound up with the physical being of man.

How does this other self work ? It has just been said that this other self belongs to the realm of Spirit, to the spiritual world ; that it is a living thought-being among living thought-beings. Among the latter, words are deeds ; and what they accomplish they effect by means of what we may, in a word, call Inspiration. The second self works inspirationally in the nature of man. What then, does it inspire ? It inspires that which we call our karma, our fate. And here we have the mysterious process :—that all we experience, whether joyous or sad, all that takes place in our lives, is inspired out of the spiritual world by our other self. If you go along the street and experience something that to you appears accidental, that is inspired out of the spiritual world by your other self. Thus there is something like inspiration in the spiritual world, and the inspiration reveals itself on the physical plane and produces the happenings which are your fate, in small things as in great. A person's fate is inspired by the other self, out of the realm of the spirit.

When this clairvoyant soul enters this realm of spirit, it experiences as a revelation in the language of spirit that whereof it can be said : words are deeds. But all that takes place in the spiritual world stamps itself upon the physical world. Whether you see a stone, a plant, a cloud, or observe the lightning, behind all these stand spiritual beings and spiritual processes. Also behind the physical processes of your own fate there stand spiritual beings and processes. Of what nature are these ? Inspirations, the occurrences of a spiritual conversation in the spiritual world ; such are used by the Cosmic Word, as the Inspirer of human fate. It is of great significance in spiritual cognition that when a man meets his other self, he ceases to think of his human personality as within the accustomed limits. He extends his Self (in which must be included the other self) over his whole fate, he expands, and then only is he truly man, when, even as he counts his finger as his own, saying, ' This belongs to me, the ego, on the physical plane,' he also says, ' It forms part of myself to give myself a bad wound or to fall, etc.' For that all comes about through the inspiration of the other self.

Now, however, we must notice in what way we meet this other self on passing the Threshold into the realm of Spirit. Over and over again we must continually recollect and put before our soul, that in all we have learned, observed, and experienced in the physical world, and even in the elementary world—in all this we have nothing that is like the characteristics of the spiritual world in which dwell the living thought-beings. So, if we were only to enter with that which we can experience in the physical world and in the elementary world, then, in the spiritual world we should be confronting nothingness. What, then, can we bring into this realm of Spirit ? Let us consider this carefully : The soul must there accustom itself not to perceive, think, feel and will as it does either in the physical or in the elementary world. That must be left behind. But it must remember what it experienced, thought, felt and willed in the physical world. As we carry over into later periods of life the memories of earlier periods, so must we carry over from the physical plane into the realm of spirit that which we have strengthened, fortified in our soul ; thus we must enter the region of Spirit with a soul that recollects the physical world.

Then we have to endure a definite experience, which may be expressed in the following words : suppose a condition were to arise in your ordinary earth-life in which all your perception ceased ; you would be able to see and hear nothing more, neither would you be able to think, feel or desire anything fresh. Every kind of life that you had so far led, ceases, and you would know only what you could remember. It is exactly in this position that you find yourself when you rise with clairvoyant consciousness into the spiritual world. There is nothing there at first which you could experience as new. You can understand it only out of your memories. Your existence consists in what has remained to you in your memories. The soul so experiences itself that it can say of itself : ' Thou art now only that which thou hast been, thy existence consists only in that which thou hast been ; present and future have now no meaning for thee, thy being consists of what thou hast been.' That is something that in certain circumstances may be easily said ; but to look upon one-self as nothing but a memory, so that one cannot experience the present, to speak of one's being as ' having-been,' is a significant experience.

When a person goes through this experience, when the clairvoyant soul penetrates as far as this, then for the first time does he begin to have a really correct understanding of Lucifer, the Being whose name has now been so often mentioned. For the human soul so rises into the spiritual world that it experiences a moment : 'Thou art only a has-been.' Lucifer is a being who, in the order of the cosmos, has come to the stage wherein he is always a 'has-been' of this kind ; he has come to be only a past, to be only the residuum of Earth-epochs that have been lived out, what bye-gone cosmic epochs have brought to his soul. And Lucifer's life—seeing that the other divine-spiritual beings who are following the normal evolution have condemned him to the past,—consists in fighting with his past against the present and the future.

Thus Lucifer stands before the clairvoyant sight ; preserving within his soul all the divine spiritual glories of the origins of the world, yet condemned to say : 'They once were within thee !' And now begins his never-ceasing struggle, to obtain for this past and present the future also in the cosmic order. When one experiences the resemblance of Lucifer, the macrocosmic resemblance of Lucifer to the microcosmic being of the human soul, on the Threshold which lies between the elementary and spiritual worlds, one experiences the whole deep tragedy of this being, Lucifer. One then begins to have a glimmering of the great cosmic mysteries which rest deep in the womb of existence, where not merely does one being struggle with another, but where ages struggle with other ages which evolve into beings, and confront one another in battle. Truly it may be said that here begins an outlook on the world wherein deep earnestness and dignity begin to pervade the soul, Here one senses something which might be called the breath of the eternal Necessities which are experienced in the Cosmic Midnight when lightnings flash across existence and in their flashing light up something like the form of Lucifer, but which die in the act of cognition and, dying, form into tokens of destiny so that they work on in the soul of man, in the form of an inner tragical karma.

The human soul itself, when it lives into the spiritual worlds, has a moment in which it is only a has-been, when it confronts the void, when it is like a point in the universe and experiences itself only as such. But this point now becomes spectator of something else. Two other things are there, to which, as a third, belongs the human soul that has become as a dot, and which at first has really nothing in itself, even as a dot has nothing in itself. The one thing that is added is that which one remembers, and that is like an external world upon which one looks back and of which one can say : 'That is what thou hast been.' When one stands there oneself without really knowing anything about oneself except this existence that is one's own past, but which one has carried across the Threshold into the spiritual world and given it living thought-being, if one

79

then has the feeling of soul-peace—then what one has carried up into the spiritual-world as one's ' has-been ' begins to hold spirit converse with the living thought-beings around it. As an objective spectator standing by, but as one who is but a point at the same time, one sees the conversation begin between the two others, one's own thought-past with the living thought-being ; they converse together. That which one has oneself carried up there, which one has made into thought, begins a spirit-conversation in the cosmic word with the spiritual living thought-being of the realm of Spirit ; there one listens to what one's own past discusses with the spiritual living being in the realm of Spirit. There one is at first like a nothing, but one is born as this nothing when one listens to the converse between one's own past and the spiritual beings in the realm of Spirit. And while one is listening, one fills oneself with new subject-matter. One now learns to recognise oneself, when one is like a point and feels oneself as such whilst one listens to the conversation between one's own past and the spiritual living being in the realm of Spirit ; and the more one can take into oneself of this spirit-conversation between one's own ' has-been ' and the future, the more does one become a spirit-being oneself.

That is the process in which, in the spiritual world, one stands within a triad. The one member of the triad is one's own ' has-been ' that one has carried up into the spirit-world, that one acquired for oneself in its spiritual form in the sense-world, and then, having crossed the Threshold, feels it as past and over. The second is the whole spiritual environment, and the third is oneself. Thus does the triad stand in the spiritual world ; and within the triad, through the opposition between the ' has-been ' and the spiritual living-being in the realm of spirit, there develops the third, the middle one, which is only like a point, but which, through listening to the spirit-conversation between the ' has-been ' and the spiritual world, increases more and more in fulness and becomes a being developing itself in the spiritual world. Thus in the spiritual world we ourselves ' become ' in clairvoyant consciousness.

That is what I wished to endeavour to describe to you in words—words which, seeing that they are necessarily borrowed from a language that belongs to the physical plane, must ever remain one-sided. But I have endeavoured as far as I can, to describe in the words of a language belonging to the physical plane, these sublime and deep relationships. For these relationships alone are capable of making a man acquainted with his true being, when he, as has been said, learns from the two others, by listening in the spiritual world. By means of such lectures as these in this course the endeavour is made to lead into the true being of man.

LECTURE 7

Munich, 30th August, 1913.

In the course of these lectures we have spoken of the ascent of clairvoyant consciousness into the worlds in which we can investigate the true being of man —a being belonging absolutely to the supersensible worlds. In the last lectures we tried to show how the human soul, when it ascends beyond the Threshold, passes first of all through the elementary world and then enters the spiritual world, when it meets with what we may call man's other self. We might also describe the ascent thus : in the first place man lives within his physical body in the physical sense-world ; when he puts aside his physical body, that is, when he goes out of it, he lives at first in his etheric body, during which time he has the elementary world as his environment. As I have already said, for the sake of those who are looking for contradictions, I shall in the final lecture draw your attention to the relation of the terms here employed to those used in my *Theosophy*. In his etheric body man lives in the elementary world around him. Then, when he lays aside his etheric body, he rises into the real spiritual world ; that is then his environment, and he lives in his astral body. In this astral body he then experiences his other self, which continues from incarnation to incarnation and concerning which we have been able to mention that in so experiencing it, we stand, as it were, before it, as a third between two other facts. We stand as a being who is simply a point over against what we may call our past, which we bring with us as memory into the spiritual world. By the fact of having carried it up there we have transformed it ; and it then begins a conversation in the region where the living thought-beings have their spiritual converse. A spirit conversation of this kind then begins, and one must, as newly born into the spiritual world, listen to that which one's own past says to the spiritual environment. This enables one to grow up and mature, as a living thought-being.

Now, there are many different things to be observed in thus growing up in the spiritual worlds. In order to acquire a good understanding of this, let us first of all take what we may call the ideal ascent into the spiritual worlds, that is, the ascent of a soul free from any sort of disturbances. We may say that such a soul hardly exists. That is just why I endeavoured to describe the spiritual path not only in a general way, but to present it dramatically as I have done, because, indeed, every soul proceeds from a personal starting-point, and consequently a normal, ideal ascent can hardly exist. Each soul has its individual spiritual path. When we take single souls such as Maria, Johannes Thomasius, Capesius, Strader, we can, of course, only show how the individual ascent takes place with each of them. But let us for a moment turn away from these ! Let us imagine how it would be if the ascent of a soul could be normally ideal, that is, if all the ideal conditions were fulfilled for crossing the Threshold, for rising into the spiritual worlds. Then, if a man were to meet his other self in the spiritual worlds, the experience would not be as though he met a photograph of himself. That which is subjective in the physical sense-world and in the elementary world, and which lives in the soul in abstract subjectivity—that which composes the soul's forces, thinking, feeling, and willing, which we believe we have in our inner being,—these are no longer within. The thinking, feeling and willing that we have in the physical world, we meet with objectively when we confront our other self in the spiritual world, and indeed as a triad. This triad which we encounter, and in presence of which we feel consciously : ' These three are myself ' I have endeavoured to present in the figures of Philia, Astrid and Luna. These figures are real ones ; they are present in the world as often as there are individual persons, individual human souls. When once they are known, one recognises them, as one recognises all grains of wheat when one has learned to know a single one. But it must be clearly understood that that which in the human soul is as a mere reflection, a faint outline, appears as a living triad, a really differentiated triad, a triad differentiated into three beings, as soon as one encounters the other self. One is oneself the Philia, Astrid and Luna. Nevertheless, these are absolutely independent living thought-beings. It is necessary to have in the fortified soul the consciousness that one is oneself the unity of these three beings. One must also be conscious that what is called thinking, feeling, and willing is an illusion, it is the shadow or image thrown into the soul by these three. An unhealthy condition of the soul might then consist, first in not recognising oneself in the spiritual world as these three beings,—that one should regard these three beings as having nothing to do with one ; or, again, if one were unable to maintain the unity and were to look upon oneself as one part Luna, another Astrid, and again, another as Philia. But to contemplate this other self as a complete triad, demands a normal, ideal course of development for the soul, such, indeed, as can hardly exist in a human soul.

If we bear in mind that which can become real in the true sense of the word, we must say that we have already pointed out that those beings whom we designate as Lucifer and Ahriman send their impulses into the physical sense-world ; we have found Ahriman and Lucifer in the most varied domains of the physical world. But when the soul of man enters upon the path of clairvoyant consciousness it comes in a much stronger and more intense degree into touch with Ahriman and Lucifer. When it passes out of the physical world and tries to penetrate into the higher worlds, Ahriman and Lucifer approach this human soul and seek to bring about many things with regard to it.

In order to understand something of the actions of Lucifer and Ahriman in this domain, we must mention the following. The human soul is, in reality, very complicated, and a person has within him many different things that contradict one another—things of which he is not master, that are in the depths of the soul without his having a true understanding of them in his ordinary con-sciousness. Now, I have already said that when a man enters the elementary world it is as though he had an experience which permits of comparison with the absurd picture of putting his head into an ant-heap ; that is, he so inserts his consciousness into the elementary world that the separate thoughts are special living thought-beings, which begin to have an independent life ; and he plunges his consciousness into this life.

Now, to the clairvoyant soul, the following becomes evident : A man always has in his soul some things of which he is not complete master, but to which he is strongly inclined. Towards such things as are connected in a special way with his inner being, Ahriman develops special activity. There are in the human soul certain parts which can, to a certain extent, be detached from the totality of the human soul. Because a man does not exercise complete control over these particular soul-contents, Ahriman gets hold of them, and owing to this activity of Ahriman (which is unjustifiable and which only arises owing to Ahriman's transgressing his limits), a tendency shows itself whereby such portions of the human etheric and also of the human astral bodies as have the inclination to sunder themselves from the rest of the soul-life and to become independent, allow themselves to be moulded by Ahriman, so that he gives them the human form. Generally speaking, any thoughts whatever which have their abode in us, can assume the human form. When man confronts these thoughts as living thought-beings, Ahriman then gets the chance of making such a portion of the human soul independent and of giving it the human form, and when man enters the elementary world, he meets with this independent portion of his being and his double. There is always one part of the human soul to which Ahriman gives the form of the human figure. We must clearly understand that when a man enters the elementary world—when he is outside his physical body, the relations of things are greatly altered. When he is within his physical body, he cannot confront himself ; but when he enters the elementary world in his etheric body, he can be in it, and yet see it from outside, as one sees one's double. This is what is meant by the double. It is, substantially, a great part of the etheric body itself. Whilst a man retains a part of the same, one portion separates itself, and becomes objective. He looks at it, it is part of his own being, to which Ahriman has given the form which he has ; for Ahriman endeavours to force everything, so to speak, into the laws of the physical world. In the physical world the Spirits of Form hold sway and share this lordship with Ahriman, so that he can very well execute with one portion of the human entity what may be designated as its transformation into the ' double.'

This meeting with the ' double ' is, comparatively speaking, a phenomenon of the elementary world which may take place through special subconscious impressions and impulses of the human soul even when a person is not clairvoyant. The following may happen : a man may be an intriguer and through his intrigues may have brought evil on many different people. One day he may have gone out and have contrived some fresh intrigue ; he comes back into his house, goes, perhaps, into his study and it may be that on his study table there lie papers on which are written things connected with the newly contrived intrigue. Now, it may befall him that, despite his normal consciousness being cynically disposed, his subconsciousness is laid hold of by that impulse to intrigue. He enters his study and there, on looking at his desk, he sees himself sitting there ! It is an unpleasant experience for a man to go through his own door, into his own room, and see himself sitting at his writing table ; but such things belong to those which often happen and, in just such a case, as that of an intriguing character, may happen very easily. That which the man meets with is truly his ' double,' whom, along with other problems, I have tried to present in *The Guardian of the Threshold* and in *The Soul's Awakening*.

We know that this ' double ' is experienced by Johannes Thomasius and there is a connection with the peculiar development of Johannes in the fact that he has this meeting with the ' double ' in the particular places shown ; because, through the remarkable experiences which he has had, Ahriman can give to a portion of his soul such a form, that the said portion is actually as a part of the etheric body, filled with the self-seeking soul-elements. This experience occurs when such preparatory conditions are created as in the case of Johannes. Through the four Mystery Plays one may get a little insight into the peculiar soul of Johannes. A certain stage of development is also indicated at the end of *The Guardian of the Threshold*. A stage of development of this kind can come about for many souls who seek the Path into the supersensible worlds.

84

Let us, then, sum up shortly how matters stand with Johannes. When we look back at *The Portal of Initiation*, we find him there experiencing, so to speak, the higher world. But how does he experience it? It may well be said that if we only take that portion of the Mystery Play contained in *The Portal of Initiation* and consider Johannes as he appears there, he does not go very far. He does not get beyond what we may call imaginative soul-experiences, with all their mistakes and one-sidednesses. What are there presented are subjective experiences, with the exception of the scenes which do not belong to the action (the introductory scene and the interlude inserted before the eighth scene). The rest are his subjective imaginative experiences. He does not progress beyond this stage in *The Portal of Initiation*. This is indicated fairly clearly in *The Portal of Initiation*, for it is shown that in all the scenes, with the exception of the two just mentioned, Johannes is always on the stage —which is somewhat difficult for the actor playing the part. We have therefore to think of everything as being in the soul of Johannes as imaginative cognition. If, too, at the end of *The Portal of Initiation* Johannes pronounces in the Temple all sorts of words that have theoretically an objective validity, it may be said that in the different Temples many persons speak words for which they are not yet mature by a long way and to which they must gradually ripen. It is not the criterion; but we recognise from the whole presentation: 'There we have to do with the subjective imaginations of Johannes.'

This already goes further in *The Soul's Probation*, wherein a higher ascent is brought about by Johannes' arriving at impressions of his earlier earth-lives— something that is not mere imagination, but where the matter extends into the objective world, where we have to do with spiritual facts which exist apart from the soul of Johannes Thomasius, as such. In *The Soul's Probation* we pass out of the subjectivity of Johannes into the objective world. So that these first two plays may be so considered that in them Johannes gradually frees himself from his inner being and goes out into the external spiritual world. Just because he goes through the first stage of his actual initiation in the course of *The Soul's Probation*, it was natural that Lucifer should acquire that misleading influence which is represented at the end of *The Soul's Probation*. Thereby we are again shown what such a soul as that of Johannes can go through, which is presented in *The Guardian of the Threshold*, where Johannes is placed in the spiritual objective world and where, certainly still impelled by his work, he at first confronts Ahriman more subjectively and takes from him what develops as something highly egotistical, in contrast to the divine order of the world.

Then begin the objective experiences in which Lucifer rules. Here we have absolutely nothing more to do with merely subjective experiences, but with the presentation of the spiritual world apart from man, which one experiences in the spiritual, just as one experiences the outer physical world in the physical. Here Johannes first enters the objective spiritual world. Hence he may still bring with him all kinds of possible errors belonging to the human soul, and, above all, his peculiar relation to Theodora. This relation must be regarded only as it is meant. We may say that Johannes enters the higher world with all the refuse of his lower self ; but he stands before the higher world and, if I may employ just an ordinary expression for this matter, I should say that he falls occultly in love with Theodora. Thus, in the relation of Johannes to Theodora, certain impulses of the physical world are carried up into the higher world.

Passing through all this, Johannes arrives at what is represented in *The Guardian of the Threshold*, at experiencing the ordinary self that belongs to the physical and elementary worlds and which, as such, we bear with us while passing through the world, and the other self which meets us on entering the spiritual world. Equally, in the ninth scene—in the Walk and also in the Temple before Hilarius—Johannes attains what may be called an inner feeling of the one self as well as of the other. But we distinctly notice that Johannes has not brought proper order into the harmony between the ordinary and the other self, in that he lives backwards and forwards in the one and then in the other self. When we consider that at the end of *The Guardian of the Threshold* and at the beginning of *The Soul's Awakening* Johannes stands there as a soul that feels within it the working of the ordinary self side by side with the other self, we understand that with him there are many things in his soul that might, so to speak, be stripped away. The ' double ' is, in the first place, separated by Ahriman ; but in another way, too, can something be separated from him.

I must emphasise the fact that I am not describing these things by way of a commentary for the Plays, but in order to use what is shown in them so as to give a presentation of really spiritual conditions and things of a spiritual nature. When we consider man's karma, the whole subjection to law of human destiny, then we must say that there is in the human soul much redeemed karma, but also much that is still unredeemed. In our past earth-lives we have gone through much that must be made good ; we have much that is not settled up, that lies, so to speak, unredeemed in the bottom of the soul—karma that has not yet been paid. Every soul has unpaid karma of this kind. Johannes Thomasius had to bring to his consciousness a very great deal of unpaid karma ; and at the moment when his inner being divides into the ordinary self and the other self much unpaid karma detaches itself. What thus separates or detaches itself is what is easily and frequently felt as separate by every soul that gradually develops to clairvoyance. A soul that does this is born, (that is, passes through birth into physical existence) in such a way that he develops the characteristics natural to a young man. We do not always find souls so disposed that they can be made into Krishnamurtis*. We live here in this world as simple children do, for their good and profit, even if later on they become clairvoyant personalities. Then at a certain point of time one can see flash forth that which also is conditioned karmically—the seeing into the spiritual worlds. But just in the case of the clairvoyant soul it frequently happens—and it is important that it should happen—if the soul has something particularly mournful or even something tragic in its disposition,—it frequently occurs that then in this clairvoyant soul there comes this vision of its own youth as an objective entity,—that youth out of which it has grown up and of which it says : ' What would have developed out of this youth, now grown almost strange to me, if I had not passed into spiritual clairvoyant conditions ? ' A kind of division of such a person then takes place. He experiences something like a kind of new birth and looks back to his youth as to another being. In this youth there lies very much whereof he says : I cannot possibly pay it all in this incarnation ; much karma lies buried there which must either be endured later, or I must exert myself to bring about its fulfilment now. There is much of this unredeemed karma in the soul of Johannes Thomasius.

Unredeemed karma—such experience as when one looks back on one's youth as upon another entity—is felt in one's inner being. To such an experience as this Lucifer has access ; it can be separated by Lucifer ; he can take a substantial part of the etheric body and can ensoul it, as it were, with unredeemed karma. This then becomes a phantom-entity, as is represented in the spirit of the young Johannes Thomasius. A phantom of this kind is a real being ; it is there detached from Johannes Thomasius, but its deeds repel because it really contradicts the general order of the cosmos. That which is outside as a phantom ought to be within Johannes Thomasius. Thereby that is evoked which one feels as a tragic fate of this phantom that lives in the elementary and spiritual worlds as part of the etheric body.

This is, therefore, the unredeemed karma of Johannes which, through Lucifer, has been made into an independent phantom-entity. He who experiences a thing of this kind—and it is an important and very significant experience—so goes through it that he knows : ' Because I have not redeemed the karma, I have contracted a kind of cosmic debt. I have created a being

* One of the unfortunate boys selected by Mrs. Besant and Leadbeater as the reincarnated Christ.

that really ought not to be outside, but within myself.' In *The Soul's Awakening* Johannes is made aware through the 'other Philia,' that he has created a soul-child of this kind, which has in certain respects an illegitimate existence outside. That is the peculiar thing, that when one raises one's life into the spiritual world, one encounters one's own being, but in spiritual objectivity this can be met with in many forms. In the case of Johannes Thomasius we have the most varied reduplications. A part of his being meets him as his double and now another part of his being—for karma belongs absolutely to the being of a person—as the spirit of the youth of Johannes Thomasius.

But now he meets yet a third ; for he is not so circumstanced that he can go through what Maria experiences. She goes through a comparatively normal development. In the ninth scene there appear to her Astrid and Luna, though not in connection with Philia, but nevertheless, two psychic forms meet her. That is a development that is approximately the normal one. It would be quite normal if Maria stood before the three figures and Thinking, Feeling, and Willing were all so objective that Maria perceived them as an unity. But development as normal as that could hardly be found. I repeat that what I endeavoured to describe are real figures ; so that the circumstances, the relations, are absolutely possible. Thus such a soul as is met by Astrid and Luna, Philia being absent—because what constitutes the consciousness-soul and intellectual soul is in Maria developed in a more regular manner than the sentient soul—such a soul goes through a development that is, to a very great extent, normal. But in Johannes Thomasius we have a development that diverges very strongly from the normal course. Here we have first of all the appearing of the 'double.' When Johannes moves towards his other self, we have the appearance of the 'double' and of the 'spirit of Johannes' youth.' That is something which belongs to the other self, and it appears multiplied because this other self appears as the illuminator of these inner conditions. And because Johannes does not draw near at once to this other self—were he to do so then all three would meet him, but he must first go through various things which pile up before him on the way to the other self—there comes to him what is still nearer to subjectivity. It is the Other Philia. The Other Philia is also in a certain sense the other self, but the other self still resting within the depths of the soul and which has not quite freed itself. It is connected with something that here, in the physical world, is likest to the spiritual world,—it is connected with the all-ruling Love, and is that which can lead one into the higher worlds because it is connected with that love. In the form of the Other Philia, a third entity approaches Johannes on the way to his other self. If a soul were to meet all three soul-forms, that soul would, so to speak, have no obstacle to encounter at all ; and in this way the whole nature of man can still objectify itself—project itself out as a complete whole into space. This is the case where the vision comes of the Other Philia in *The Soul's Awakening* at the end of Scene 2.

Now I have told you how when a person becomes an inmate of the elementary world—and certain characteristics of that life remain, even when the person raises himself beyond, into the spiritual world,—he must acquire the faculty for transformation ; because in the spiritual world everything is in a state of transformation, for there is no definite form. Form is only in the physical world. In the elementary world there is movement, the faculty for transformation. But in connection with this we also find that because all is in a continual state of transformation, confusions may occur when one is met by anything of the nature of an entity. Everything is in continual transformation. If one does not immediately grasp it, so to say, one confuses it with another. That is what happens to Johannes when he first sees the Other Philia before him and takes the ' double ' for her. Such mistakes may easily occur. We must clearly understand that one first has to work through to the true vision of the higher worlds, and that just there, owing to the transformative faculty, confusion may very easily occur. The way in which these mistakes show themselves is particularly significant for the course taken in the development of a soul. You remember that Johannes has an experience three times. That he has this experience in the way he does depends on the fact that he has evolved in a certain way. The first experience is with the Other Philia, the second with his Double, and the third with the Other Philia again. Here we have a triad of experiences. We have generally to do with triads in the world. In fact, we must seek out these triads, for they are always there. That Johannes Thomasius twice sees the Other Philia before him, once only the Double, and once confuses the two,—this is connected with what he has attained. The fact that he perceives this soul-child, as we might say, the Spirit of the Young Johannes which is his own creation, though brought about with the help of Lucifer, but which exists out there in the cosmos—that is also connected with what he himself is.

It is often one of the most agitating experiences of clairvoyant consciousness, to find that parts of one's karma which have not yet been balanced, have, through Lucifer, been made independent as phantom-beings in the spiritual world. Many such phantoms may be found, which, through our unpaid karma, we have under the influence of Lucifer transposed into the spiritual world. These experiences with the phantoms correspond with the soul's stage of development. Suppose matters lay differently with Johannes and that he made a mistake twice over ; that he twice saw incorrectly and once correctly, or that he twice saw the Double and once only the Other Philia. Johannes is still too much trammelled with subjectivity; Maria is already so strong on the objective side that two soul-forces come before her. Johannes must still so fortify his soul that he may be met by that which as yet remains fairly subjective ; 'magical weaving of thine own being,'—that becomes objective. With these words he also strengthens his soul, with the words : ' Magical weaving of thine own being.' And when this magic web of his own being comes up and approaches the other self, Johannes stands before himself as his Double, as the Spirit of the Young Johannes, as the Other Philia. Johannes would have a different nature if he were to experience the triad otherwise, if he—let us say—were to make the mistake twice and could twice experience his Double. If that were the case, then Johannes would be another person. If the matter were not as is represented in *The Soul's Awakening*, Johannes would not look upon one spirit of the young Johannes, but on many such in the realm of shadows. If in the place of Johannes Thomasius you were to imagine a Johannes who was to make a mistake twice, or could twice experience the 'Double,' then there would have to be many Spirits of the Young Johannes, then there would have to be many such soul-children of Johannes. In such matters as these we touch the hem of great psychic mysteries.

From all that I have set before you, you see that it is a complicated path, this path of the clairvoyant soul to the true being of man ; that this human soul is a complicated being, and that in rising into the spiritual world a person gradually approaches his true being, when he himself becomes a memory-being, a ' has-been,' when for the human soul there comes the consciousness : ' Thou art not now in the present, thou hast also at present no future before thee—thou art that which thou hast been ; thou bearest thy past into the present.' He grows further as spiritual being when the past that he has carried up into the spiritual world and which he spiritually experiences, begins to hold converse with the surrounding spiritual world. He grows by listening to this conversation of his own past with the living thought-beings of the spiritual world. But while thus feeling himself transposed into the spiritual world in which he finds his other self, he always has an experience which may be expressed somewhat in the following manner. We may say that a man feels : Thou art, indeed, now in the spiritual world, and since thou dwellest there in thine astral body thou canst find thine other self as a spiritual being ; but thy really true being—that which thou really art—that thou canst not find as yet even in this world. That whereof thine ego in the physical world is the phantom form, thou dost not yet find, despite thine ascent into the spiritual world. Then he learns little by little what an important experience he must still have in order to find the true ego, the true inner being, which is still ensheathed in this other self.

The human entity is indeed complicated, and lies deep, deep down below, in the depths of the soul, and in order to reach the true ego many and various experiences must be gone through. We have described much of what a man must go through in order to reach his true self which lives within him. In order to come to the true ego, the following has also to be experienced. We have laid stress on how one penetrates into the spiritual world with one's memory, how at first one has no new impressions, but must allow that to speak which one has been in the past : how, as a dot-like entity, one must listen to the spirit conversation between one's own ' has-been ' and the spiritual world around : this memory remains with one. It remains with one also between death and a new birth. It is just that which one has been, that is present first of all in the spiritual world. The memory of the real sense-existence between birth and death remains firmly settled and it remains in the soul between death and a new birth. But if, as a soul that has become clairvoyant, a person wishes to penetrate to the true ego, he learns to recognise that a decision, a spiritual act, is necessary. Of this it must be said that there must be a strong decision in the will to obliterate within himself, to forget within himself, that which he has brought into the spiritual world as a memory of himself ; a decision of the will to obliterate the memory of what he has been, with all its details. Then he comes to something that can also be dimly perceived even at earlier stages of clairvoyance and cognition. An earlier announcement of what is thus experienced in the spiritual world is presented in the third scene of *The Soul's Awakening* where Strader confronts the abyss of his being. A person only stands really before the abyss of existence, when he makes the decision through free inner willing, through an energetic act of the will, to extinguish, to forget himself.

In reality, all these things exist as facts in the human being, only he knows nothing of them. Every night man must unconsciously obliterate himself in this way. But it is a very different thing to hand over in full consciousness one's memory-ego to destruction and oblivion, and really to stand for a while in the spiritual world at the edge of the abyss of being, as a nullity, confronting the void. It is the most terrifying experience that one can have ; and yet one must approach it with the greatest confidence. In order to go to the abyss as a nullity it is necessary to have the confidence that the true ego will be brought to one out of the Cosmos. And that does occur. When one has brought about this forgetting on the brink of the abyss of being, one knows :—Extinguished is all that thou hast so far experienced ; thou thyself hast extinguished it, but out of another world which thou hast hitherto not known,—I might say, a super-spiritual world,—thy true ego, which was still ensheathed in the other self, comes to thee. Now only and for the first time, after having completely extinguished oneself, does one meet one's true ego, of which the ego in the physical world is but the phantom form, the Maya. For the true ego of man belongs to the super-spiritual world, and man belongs to that world with his true ego, of which the physical ego is but a faint shadow.

Thus, the ascent into the super-spiritual world is an inner experience. It is the experience of a completely new world at the edge of the abyss of being, and the reception of the true ego from this super-spiritual world, on the brink of the abyss of existence.

I wanted to lay within your souls this description, as a connecting bridge between this lecture and the next. In a way it should occupy our thoughts as a connecting link until to-morrow's lecture when we shall speak further of what I have said to-day concerning the meeting at the abyss of existence.

LECTURE 8

Munich, 31st August, 1913.

In such a course of lectures as this which we are now about to finish, thoughts easily come into our minds which here or there may point to what may be called the ' civilisation ' of the present day. In many details of various kinds we have had to call attention to the remarkable way in which the Ahri-manic and Luciferic forces interplay in this present-day civilisation. Now anyone who with unbiassed feeling and some understanding of spiritual science accustoms himself to a kind of objective consideration of the present-day civilisation, must doubtless feel the confusion, the chaos of the same. For years it has been my custom to direct attention as little as possible to this, but rather to employ our time in contributing in as positive a manner as we can to the opening up of the spiritual worlds. But although we shall make no great departure from this custom of ours, yet we may and must, now and always, emphasise the fact that through this self-chosen moderation—the expression is certainly not employed in any presumptuous spirit—many misunderstandings have crept in during the whole course of our efforts and our work. From just the standpoint that is ours, two things are necessary : first to acquire a correct objective understanding of the fact that though certainly the evolution, the development, of the Post-Atlantean world has brought about the chaotic, confused, and to some extent inferior and second-rate condition of modern civilisation of humanity in its widest circles, yet up to a certain point, this has been a necessity. We must rightly and objectively understand that mere criticism is not sufficient for these things—we need the understanding of them. On the other hand, it is necessary to meet this confused and chaotic element in the intellectual and spiritual life of the day, with clear and open sight, in so far as one adopts the point of view rendered accessible through Spiritual Science. For again and again I have had the experience that some of the well-meaning and the best-intentioned of our friends come and tell me that in some place or other something really theosophical has appeared ; and again and again I have had to convince myself how inferior these so-called theosophical things are.

As I have said, I do not wish to depart from my usual custom, but I should like to point out, as an example, at the close of these lectures, a single and specially ridiculous phenomenon. Certain persons are bringing themselves much to the fore at present who pose to the world with a certain assumption of learning, without even the very least understanding of their subject ; and those who have not been accustomed to employ their powers of discrimination may, given the opportunity, be very easily carried away with high-sounding words. That is something that must gradually disappear from among us. We must acquire for ourselves a power of clear, objective discrimination. By this means we should then have a more correct view than we so far have had of the relation in which those inferior currents and personalities stand with regard to our own movement—a thing to be desired.

. . . .

Such currents as these come up under many and various conditions, and I should like to mention one such, and this not in order to criticise or bring forward anything connected with opposition towards our work, but simply to characterise it objectively. There has appeared from a Berlin publishing house an edition of *The Chymical Marriage of Christian Rosenkreuz* and other works by Christian Rosenkreuz. It is obvious that many of our friends, or other persons interested in occult movements, would easily be attracted to a new edition like this, of works which have always been difficult to obtain. Now in this *Chymical Marriage of Christian Rosenkreuz* there is a preface, which really surpasses everything imaginable in grotesque learning—I prefer to avoid a more explicit description. Let me read merely a few lines from this preface without entering further into what is said in other passages. It says : ' When we approach occult science with critical and exact methods (those are words by which many people are misled), one will very soon become aware that from this point one can easily get a feeling towards the two-afore-mentioned poles.' (I shall not discuss what the poles are to which the author alludes, all that is only—well, I would rather forego any more exact designation.) ' For this the newly formulated concept of Allomatics is specially good, as under its guidance one easily becomes master of all difficulties that approach from both sides.' (Allomatics is something that greatly impresses many people.) ' Allomatics is the teaching, science, and philosophy of the Other, derived from the Greek " allos," the other, as opposed to the ego,—the nothingness and non-existence of the ego. Everything comes from the non-ego . . . in short, from the Other.' —And this erudition goes on further. Now, this learning with which one is prepared for the *Chymical Marriage of Christian Rosenkreuz*—really I do not wish to say this out of animosity, but from objective logic—is absolutely the same as though one were to lay the foundation of an apple or ' Pear-ology ' or a

'Pearomatics' instead of Xenology and Allomatics. With exactly the same logic as that of this strange fellow, who derives the world from the ego and the non-ego, one can trace back the world to a pear and everything that is not this pear, the other of this pear; and one can employ exactly the same words and concepts to explain the whole world from pear and non-pear. According to a man like this, there would be nothing omitted from the world and its phenomena if, instead of explaining them by Ego and the Other, one explains them according to pear-ology and pear-omatics, a doctrine of the pear and the other-of-the-pear. That presents itself as a learned work, it employs all sorts of comparisons from embryology in order to appear to be a learned work; it speaks almost in the same tone as do many of our own so-called learned works which are taken as serious, and which—and I repeat that this is said without animosity, in fact, in complete brotherhood—are often honestly received by our friends as though they were something, whereas they are only the products of the inferiority of our age. That implies a very small amount of the capacity of discrimination for what possesses real value, and for nonsense which stands on such a level of literature as this. Hence it can be said with complete objectivity: If such a person is just one of those who brought out or repeated the foolish Jesuit fable,* then one can also form an idea of the value of the opposition which has lately made itself felt against us from all sides. The chief point in question is that one should get a right attitude to that which, just in occultism, creeps out from all the corners of the world, and yet which is taken by many as of equal significance with earnestly meant Spiritual Science. The thing is that if one wants to be an honest disciple of Spiritual Science one must acquire a correct feeling with regard to these gentlemen. And this feeling is, that it is best to ignore them instead of pampering and encouraging them in everything they produce; that one knows, one should really advise them to use the time they take in writing such stuff as this in doing something more profitable for humanity, for example, in doing fret-work. That would be far more useful to humanity than writing nonsense of this kind. It is necessary for us to look at such things with complete objectivity, and really to accustom ourselves to appraise at its true worth the civilisation of the present day with all its ingredients. If we have only the right thoughts and feelings about these things and personalities, then we, too, shall come out all right. We must clearly understand one thing, namely, that such phenomena as these of the present day are certainly explicable on the other side; for we have seen how Ahrimanic and Luciferic forces penetrate into the evolution of human civilisation.

* Mrs. Besant's attack on Dr. Steiner.

As we have frequently pointed out, just as everything in the impulses that interplay in the evolution of humanity changes from one epoch to another, so also do the Ahrimanic and Luciferic impulses. Our epoch is in a certain sense a reversed repetition of the Egyptian-Chaldean age, but because it is a reversed repetition, the Luciferic and Ahrimanic forces play, on the whole, another rôle from that in the ancient Egyptian-Chaldean Age. During the latter, the human soul could look out on what was happening and could say : From the one side come the Ahrimanic, from the other the Luciferic influences. In the Egyptian civilisation the distinction could still be very well made. In the Græco-Latin age of civilisation things had already gone so far that Lucifer and Ahriman met directly before the human soul and balanced each other. Anyone who enters more deeply into the real fundamental nature of the Græco-Latin civilisation can observe this state of balance between Lucifer and Ahriman. In our time it has already become different. Lucifer and Ahriman now make a pact, so to speak, in the outer world ; they knot together their impulses in the external world before these impulses reach the human soul ; so that we have the tangle, the knot, within the development of our civilisation, whereas in olden times the threads of the Ahrimanic and Luciferic impulses were quite separate. It is now quite difficult for man to undo the knots, to find a way out of the tangle. Everywhere in our movement of civilisation we have the Ahrimanic and Luciferic threads interlacing one with another, and we shall not get a sound view of the conditions of our civilisation until we realise that in many of our agitations and social movements, yea, in very many of the abstract ideas and external arrangements to be met with, not merely now but in the future, we have the tangled threads of the Luciferic and Ahrimanic impulses. We must be watchful concerning these threads and exercise vigilance over that which belongs to Lucifer and Ahriman, interwoven in such motley confusion—that is what we must bear in mind.

No one is better able to understand and deal with this Luciferic and Ahrimanic element than one who tries to pursue the path of spiritual knowledge, and to equip his soul with clairvoyant powers in order that the real being of man which he cannot know in his ordinary consciousness may become unveiled and the object of true Spiritual Science. It will be evident, from the representations that have been given, that as soon as a man enters the higher worlds he has, in a certain sense, to pass over a Threshold. In so far as he is still an earth-being and has, nevertheless, made his soul clairvoyant, he must pass backwards and forwards over this Threshold, and must know how to conduct himself in the spiritual world beyond the Threshold just as well as in the physical world on this side of it. Both in the lectures and also repeatedly in our Mystery Plays, attention has been drawn to an important experience—the experience of the Threshold, the so-called meeting with the Guardian of the Threshold.

As has already been mentioned, one can most certainly ascend into the spiritual worlds and experience various things there without having this, in one sense terrifying, and in another, most highly important and significant experience with the Guardian of the Threshold. But for a clear objective vision of the spiritual worlds it is of infinite importance that one should have had this meeting with him at some time. In my brochure, *The Threshold of the Spiritual World*, I have indicated all that is connected with this, as far as is possible in a work that treats these things in an aphoristic manner. Many things I have added thereto in the course of these lectures. I should like now to add a few more details to this description of *The Guardian of the Threshold*—for if I were to describe the meeting with him in full detail I should have to give a long cycle of lectures on the subject.

I want you to notice that when a man first leaves his physical body—in which he has the physical world as his environment—he enters the elementary world ; and then, while he is surrounded by the elementary world, he lives in his etheric body, as in the physical world he lives in the physical body. If he then passes clairvoyantly out of the etheric body, he lives in the astral body and has around him the spiritual world. We have pointed out that a man can also pass out of his astral body and be in his true ego. Then he has for his environment the super-spiritual world. When he passes into these worlds he at last reaches his true ego which he has always had in the depths of his soul ; whereas before, while in the spiritual world, he found the way in which the true ego, the other self reveals itself there ; namely, enveloped in living thought-essence.

All of us who are going about on the physical plane have in us this other self, but the ordinary consciousness can know nothing about the fact that one only experiences the essential entity of this other self, this true ego, when one ascends into the spiritual and super-spiritual worlds. In reality we always carry about within us this true ego, as our unfailing companion. But this true ego which we meet at the Threshold of the spiritual world is present in a peculiar manner—I might say, in a peculiar garb. On the Threshold of the spiritual world this true ego can robe itself in all that constitutes our weaknesses, our failings, in all that makes us prone—so to speak—to remain attached with our whole being to the physical sense-world, or at least to the elementary world.

Thus we meet with our own true ego on the Threshold of the spiritual worlds. Abstract Theosophy can very easily say : ' This other self, this true ego—why, that is ourselves !' As regards the essential reality, this statement that we ourselves are the true ego is not of much significance. We certainly all of us go about in the spiritual worlds as our other self ; but we are really another. When with our consciousness we linger in the physical world, this other self of ours is very different,—something foreign to us, a being we encounter as truly much more foreign to us than any other person in the earth-world. And this other self, this true ego, clothes itself in our weaknesses, in all that we really should forsake and do not want to forsake because, as a matter of habit, we remain attached to it as physical sense-men when we want to pass over the Threshold. Thus we really meet on the Threshold of the spiritual world a spiritual being differing from all the other spirit-beings we may meet with in the supersensible worlds. All other spiritual beings appear, more or less, with coverings that are more suited to their nature than is the case with those of the Guardian of the Threshold. He clothes himself in that which not only arouses in us trouble and anxiety, but often horror and loathing ; he clothes himself in our weaknesses, in that of which we may say : 'We tremble with fear lest we should not get away from it,' or, 'We not only blush, but are almost overcome with shame when we look at what we are, that in which the Guardian of the Threshold is clad.' Thus it is indeed a meeting with oneself, but truly also the meeting with another being.

Now one does not easily get past the Guardian of the Threshold. We may say that to obtain some sort of vision of the spiritual worlds is easy in comparison with getting what is correct and true. Especially at the period in which we are now living it is not so very difficult to get some sort of impression of the spiritual world ; but to enter the spiritual worlds so that one sees them as they really are, it is necessary, particularly if one's encounter with the Guardian of the Threshold has been perhaps delayed until comparatively late, that one must have prepared oneself well beforehand, in order that when one does have it, one may experience it properly. Most people, or at least very many, get as far as the Guardian of the Threshold. But the point is that we should come to him consciously. Unconsciously we stand before him every night. The Guardian of the Threshold is, in reality, a great benefactor in that he does not allow himself to be seen, for people could not endure the sight of him. That which we experience every night unconsciously would mean, if it were brought to our knowledge, the meeting with the Guardian of the Threshold. Generally speaking, people get as far as the boundary where, so to speak, the Guardian stands. In such a moment as this, however, something strange happens to the soul, and it may be said that the soul experiences it in a dreamy state between consciousness and unconsciousness. The soul has the tendency on the border line to see herself, as she is, as she clings to the physical world with all her weaknesses and failings ; but she cannot bear it, and before the whole process can reach her consciousness, through the horror that she feels, she deadens, as it were, her consciousness ; and such moments as these, in which the soul deadens her consciousness, are the best points of attack for the Ahrimanic beings. As a fact, we get through to the Guardian of the Threshold when our feeling of self has been developed with special force and strength. We must strengthen this feeling of self if we want to rise up into the spiritual world. With the strengthening of this feeling of self strength comes also to all the inclinations and habits, weaknesses and prejudices, which are otherwise kept back within their limits by our up-bringing, by custom, and by external civilisation. On the Threshold of the spiritual world the Luciferic impulses assert themselves strongly from within ; and as the human soul has the tendency to deaden herself, Lucifer at once unites with Ahriman, with the consequence that the entrance is barred to the spiritual world.

If a man seeks, with a healthy soul, for knowledge of Spiritual Science and does not live in a state of unhealthy craving for spiritual experiences, nothing specially unpleasant can take place at the boundary. If he conforms to all that has to be conformed to in real, true Spiritual Science, nothing else happens than that, in a certain way, Lucifer and Ahriman balance each other for the striving soul at the Threshold of the spiritual world. But when there is a special craving to get in, then things come to such a pass that that really happens of which one can say : ' The person pilfers, partakes on the sly, in the spiritual world.' And that which he has pilfered is densified by Ahriman, so that what would otherwise have no entrance pushes itself into the consciousness of the person ; the latter then experiences in the densified condition what he has pilfered in the spiritual world, where it so confronts him that it appears exactly after the pattern of physical impression. In short, he has hallucinations, illusions, and thinks he stands before a spiritual world because he has come as far as the Guardian of the Threshold ; but he has not gone past him, rather has he been thrown back with his pilferings from the spiritual world. What he thus enjoyed on the sly is condensed to that which can perfectly well contain true pictures of the spiritual world, but does not contain the most important part, that whereby the soul may have a clear view concerning the truth and the value of what it sees.

In order to pass the Guardian of the Threshold aright, it is absolutely necessary to develop self-knowledge—real, genuine, unsparing self-knowledge. Not to wish to enter the spiritual worlds when karma makes it possible to do so in one's incarnation, is a neglect of one's duty towards the progress of evolution.

It would be quite wrong to say to oneself, ' I shall not enter the spiritual worlds, for fear of making mistakes.' We should strive as intensely as we can to enter ; but, on the other hand, we must clearly understand that we may not shrink back from that before which a man is most apt and willing to shrink, that is, real, true self-knowledge. On this point one experiences many things. Nothing is really so difficult in life for a human being as real self-knowledge. We can experience many a thing that is grotesque, remarkable, in this respect. We may meet people who, in their upper consciousness, are continually emphasising that they do this or that from completely unselfish motives, that they want nothing, nothing at all for themselves. When we understand such souls, we often find that though they imagine it is so, yet in their subsconsciousness they are thorough egoists and only want what suits their own ego. We may find people who, from their upper consciousness, let us say, make speeches, use words, write books, and in a few comparatively short pages we may find such words as ' love,' and ' tolerance,' mentioned eighteen to twenty-five times, without the very slightest trace of that love or tolerance being in their souls as an actual fact. There is nothing in which we can be so easily deceived as about ourselves, if we do not always, again and again, take care to exercise a genuine, honest self-knowledge. But it is intensely difficult to exercise this self-knowledge directly. It has, indeed, happened that persons have so shut themselves off from self-knowledge, that, rather than admit what they are at the present time, they prefer to admit having been apes during the moon evolution :* so great can be the delusion with regard to the duty of true, genuine self-knowledge. It would be a good exercise for many a one who is striving towards the domain of the spirit if, from time to time, he would practise the following : if he said to himself : ' I shall think back over the last three or four weeks, or, better still, months ; I shall let important facts, my various deeds, pass in review before my mental eyes. I shall quite systematically look away from all that may have happened to me of an unjust nature. I shall entirely eliminate all that I usually so frequently say in excuse for what has happened to me, that is : that it is the other's fault. I shall never think that any other than myself can be to blame.' If we reflect how easily a human being is in-clined constantly to make someone else rather than himself or herself answer-able, we shall be able to judge what a good plan such a review of life is, where one has suffered some injustice and yet knowingly eliminates the thought of this injury and does not allow the criticism to arise that the other one might have been wrong. We should practise such an exercise, and we shall see that

* Referring to the book, *Man : Whence, How and Whither,* by Mrs. Besant and Mr. Leadbeater.

thereby we inwardly gain quite a different relation to the spiritual world. Practices such as these change much in the real disposition, the true inward state of the human soul.

When seeking the path to the clairvoyant soul, the extreme difficulty of entering the higher worlds without danger, so to speak, shows, as we have said repeatedly, that it is necessary not to lose oneself when one has to put one's head into the ant-heap. A strengthened feeling of self is necessary, a feeling of self that a person must not develop in the physical world, if he does not want to be a hardened egoist. But if he wants to maintain himself in the higher worlds, if he wants to experience, to realise himself there, he must enter those worlds with an enhanced feeling of self. But, on coming back into the sense-world, he must also have the faculty for eliminating this feeling of self so that down here he may not be a thorough-going egoist. Thus, yonder, in the other worlds, we must have a strengthened feeling of self. That can be taken to mean that in order to live in the higher worlds of spiritual things we need a strengthened feeling of self ; but, on the other hand, we require the opposite of the statement just made—the knowledge that we must indeed find, in the spiritual world, the strengthened feeling of self,—but in the physical world the spirit manifests itself in a special manner in what we may call, in the widest sense in the physical world, Love, the capacity for love, the capacity for sympathy, sharing both joys and sorrows.

He who learns clairvoyantly to experience the higher powers knows that what Maria says in *The Soul's Awakening* is correct, that is, that in reality the ordinary sense-consciousness which man has on the physical plane is a kind of sleep, as compared with what he feels and experiences in the higher worlds, and that the entering into the higher worlds is an awakening. It is quite correct and true to say that in the physical world men sleep in comparison with the experiencing of the higher worlds, and that it is only because they are always asleep that they do not feel the sleep. If, then, when the clairvoyant soul crosses the Threshold into the spiritual worlds, what it experiences there is an awakening with a strengthened feeling of self ; on the other hand, the awakening of the self is brought about in the physical world by love, that love which was described in one of the first lectures, as ' the love which exists for the sake of the characteristics and attributes of the beloved is the form of love which is protected from the Luciferic and Ahrimanic influences '; it is that love which, in the physical sense-world, is really under the influence of the good and progressing Powers of existence. The effect of this kind of love is clearly shown in the experiences of clairvoyant consciousness. What we develop in the way of egoism in the physical world, and concerning which we are so unwilling to acquire self-knowledge, shows itself when it is brought up into the spiritual worlds. Nothing is so disturbing, no experience is so hard and embittering as what we carry up as the result of the lovelessness and lack of feeling which we develop in the physical world. When, through the clairvoyant soul, we ascend into the spiritual world, we feel very much upset by all the lovelessness and selfishness we have developed in the physical sense-world. When we thus cross the Threshold, everything shows itself ; not only the open but the hidden egoism that rages in the depths of men's souls. And while they are giving themselves up to the dream that they are selfless, a man who manifests an external egoism, frankly owning that he will have this or that, is perhaps much less egoistic than those who manifest out of theosophical abstractions a certain egoistic selflessness in their upper consciousness, especially when they declaim about this selflessness in all sorts of oft and oft repeated expressions about love and tolerance. The lovelessness and want of sympathy thus carried up into the higher world, transforms itself into hideous and frequently terrifying forms which we experience when we enter the spiritual worlds. These are truly very disturbing, very disagreeable for the soul.

And then there comes one of those moments that are very significant, and which must be considered when we speak of the knowledge and experiences of higher worlds. If a person is full of courage and pluck it would be best for him, as soon as he goes into the higher worlds and gets into a sphere of disagreeable things, to look these calmly in the face, and quietly own to himself : ' Well, now, thou art carrying so much egoism up into the higher worlds . . . it would be best, bravely, freely, and frankly to confront this egoism of thine.' But the human soul has generally the tendency to cast these disagreeables off, so to speak, before becoming thoroughly conscious of them ; to kick out left and right as horses do, and get rid of these unpleasant things. The moment the results of egoism are thrown off Lucifer and Ahriman have an easy game with the human soul ; in their compact they can very easily lead the soul of man into their special kingdom, where they can place before it all sorts of spiritual worlds which the human being then looks upon as the true, real, spiritual worlds, grounded in the cosmic order. We may say that the development of true, real love, earnest and honourable sympathy, are both good preparations for the soul which aspires to rise with clear vision into the spiritual worlds. That which has been said is not quite unnecessary and will be understood by anyone who reflects a little on the difficulty of attaining true sympathy and capacity for love in the world.

Herewith we have described several things connected with the crossing of the Threshold into the spiritual worlds. When this relation of man to the spiritual worlds is described, we must clearly understand that real, genuine knowledge of the nature of man can only be attained through such descriptions as these ; for through these alone can we know what man in actual truth is, and thereby alone can we come into relation with that which, in a natural but somewhat altered manner, places a human being before the higher, the spiritual worlds, that is, in the periods which he goes through between death and a new birth.

At this point I must, in a few words, point to that which I have already explained in the last chapter of my booklet, *The Threshold of the Spiritual World*. We know from earlier descriptions given in my books *Theosophy* and *Occult Science* that man, when he passes through the Gate of Death, lays aside his physical body, and then still has his etheric body about him, for a time that may perhaps only last for a few days. Then he also lays this aside. Now we may say : When a man has put aside this etheric body he is then at first in his astral body. Thus the soul goes through a sort of further journeying with the astral body. The etheric body is laid aside ; it has a destiny which is dependent on the world into which it is transposed, which is the elementary world. In this elementary world—as we have been able to explain—the dominant quality is that of transformation. Everything is undergoing perpetual transformation. Without the man's soul being present, therefore, the etheric body is handed over to the elementary world, and, separated from that human soul, goes through its fate of transformation in the elementary world. Then in the years which for some last a longer, for others a shorter time, the man lives in his astral body, and he lives in what, from the point of view of clairvoyant consciousness, may be called the Elementary World. But there is quite a definite tendency in the soul after death—in the period immediately following death. In the physical world man is not so conditioned as to be continually looking at his own stomach, liver, spleen, he cannot do it. He does not see into his own body ; it is not his habit, on the physical plane, to direct his gaze into his own body but upon his environment. But when he has passed the Portal of Death and lives through the time which in my *Theosophy* is called the Soul World, the exact contrary is the case. When the soul has the natural tendency to turn its gaze principally upon the fate of its own etheric body. The transformations which the etheric body goes through in the elementary world form, to a certain extent throughout the whole period of kamaloca, the environment, the external world of the soul. During this time we see how the elementary world receives our etheric body. If a man has been a good-natured fellow here on the physical plane, he sees how the ' good-nature ' accommodates itself to the laws of the elementary world ; if he has been an ill-natured fellow, he sees how little his etheric body (the part of it that was concerned with his ill-nature) can accommodate itself to the laws of the elementary world ; how everywhere this etheric body, which he has, indeed, laid aside and which has become the sole object of his attention, is on all sides rejected. The experiences of kamaloca consist in our seeing what we have been, by the changing fate of our etheric body.

We need not find fault with Anthroposophy for teaching this, for Aristotle and others taught much more besides. They taught, for instance, that this retrospect lasted an eternity,—this review of one's own fate—so that while perhaps a man had lived on earth for eighty or ninety years, he must look on during an eternity at what he had accomplished on his own etheric body. The truth is what Anthroposophy teaches, namely, that this vision of the etheric body and its fate, brought about by what one has been, lasts one, two, or three decades. That is the environment ; it is composed of the transformations in the elementary world, chiefly of such beings as are similar to man's own etheric body, chiefly of the etheric body of man himself. If you want a more graphic description of these matters take what I have described in my *Theosophy* as the passage of the soul through the soul-world.

If we want to describe the spiritual worlds at all properly, we must not pedantically keep our concepts rigid in a way which may be useful enough for the physical world ; we must clearly understand that during our kamaloca period our whole environment is dependent on the mood of the soul. On this depends the fact that what has to be described as the elementary world adapts itself to the soul-world ; one sees chiefly the etheric part becoming dissolved in the elementary world. This dissolving etheric can be described stage for stage as is done in my *Theosophy*.

Then comes the time in which something enters, as it were, in the period between death and a new birth, something that, in the clairvoyant consciousness of which we have been speaking, has to be brought about to a certain extent artificially. After man has laid aside his etheric body he lives in his astral body ; then also begins a period in which the astral body detaches itself from the true ego, in which one then lives on for a further period. But this process of detachment takes place in a special manner. It does not come about as a snake would slip off its skin, but this astral body becomes looser on all sides ; it continually grows larger and larger and incorporates itself in the whole sphere. In so doing it becomes thinner and thinner and is, as it were, absorbed by the whole surrounding world. At first one stands, so to speak, in the middle of one's own spiritual surroundings. On all sides the astral body loosens itself and is absorbed in all directions, so that the environment a man has about him after death, after the astral body has loosened itself, consists of the spiritual world and of that which is absorbed from his own astral body. He thus sees his own astral body gradually go forth. At the same time it becomes, of course, less and less distinct, because it grows larger and larger. He also feels himself within this astral body, as has been said in many lectures, and yet again separate from it. These things are extremely difficult to describe. In order to get a picture of it, suppose that you see a whole swarm of gnats together—a swarm consisting of a great many gnats,—when you see it from the distance it looks like a black ball. When the single gnats fly away on all sides, there is soon nothing more to be seen of it. So it is with the astral body. When it is being absorbed by the whole cosmic sphere it becomes more and more indistinct, we see it dispersing in the world until it is lost. With this astral body we lose that which is always present when we have gone through the Gate of Death—what we may call our 'past,' the being connected with what we have experienced on the physical plane in the physical and etheric bodies. We see our own being losing itself as it were, in the spiritual world. It is an experience similar to the one created voluntarily by one who is aiming at the discovery of his true ego in the spiritual world. This terrifying and significant impression which a person can have when he treads the path of clairvoyant consciousness takes place naturally in the manner we have described, and a real forgetting occurs sooner, the less the soul, after death, turns out to have been strengthened and fortified. Selfless unegoistic souls that are often described as weak in physical life are precisely the souls that are strong after death ; they can see for a long time that which they have brought in memory, from physical existence, into the spiritual world. The so-called strong egoists are the puny ones of the spiritual world, their own astrality disappears very soon, when it gradually dissolves like a sphere into the spiritual world.

There really comes a moment when all that one can remember disappears. It returns, but now in an altered manner. All is again brought back that had disappeared; it gathers together again, but so that it shows what it must become, in consequence of what had departed, so that the proper, new life, conformably with karma, may build itself up in accordance with the old earth-life. Thus from infinity there draws in again towards a central point what must be given to us, what must return, to our consciousness from oblivion, so that we may construct our new life according to our karma. Thus a kind of forgetting, an experiencing of nothing but oneself in the true ego, takes place somewhere about the middle of the period between death and a new birth.

Most human souls of to-day are only so far prepared that they experience this forgetting in a sort of spiritual sleep of the soul ; but those who are prepared for it, experience just in this moment of forgetting, of the transition from the memory of the preceding earth-life to the preparation for the coming one, that which in *The Soul's Awakening* is called the Cosmic Midnight ; wherein one can enter deeply into the necessities of existence. This picture of the Cosmic Midnight is connected with the deepest mysteries of human existence. Thus we may say : That which man mysteriously is, or that which is his true nature wherein he lives between death and a new birth and which can never be experienced through the ordinary consciousness, discloses itself to the clairvoyant soul. And this experience of the absorption of one's own astrality by the spiritual surroundings and which we have on this occasion described from the standpoint of clairvoyant consciousness, can be exactly described, stage for stage, as is done in my books *Theosophy* and *Occult Science*, as the actual spirit-land. What the soul experiences when in the natural course there comes about that which is brought about artificially through the experiences that have been described for the clairvoyant consciousness, can be described as is done in my book *Theosophy*. There you have the agreement of the expressions which are here used for these conditions, with those which are employed in the books *Theosophy* and *Occult Science*.

Thus we can say that we have endeavoured both in this course of lectures and in the Mystery Plays, to point to the nature of the Cosmos and to that which shares in that nature, that is, the entity of man. After such observations as these have been offered, perhaps it may also be added that it will be necessary to pursue a little more with one's own soul such paths as have been pointed out in these lectures. For you will see, if you seek to penetrate more and more deeply into *The Soul's Awakening* that many a thing connected with the mysteries of existence will so dawn upon you that you will say : ' These things are really there for the revealing and unveiling of these mysteries.' I call your attention, for example, to the following : Try to go through, in further meditation, what I have said about Ahriman as the Lord of Death in the world, in connection with what is represented in *The Soul's Awakening*. It is clearly shown from the beginning of the third scene, but it was already hinted at in the words that Strader speaks to the manager of the works, that : ' What is to happen will happen ' . . . in which words the manager hears something like whisperings from the spiritual world—and through these whisperings his spiritual discipleship begins. It is more or less hinted at there ; but from the third scene onwards we see gradually more and more clearly the moods, the forces, which prepare the death of Strader. We shall not understand why in the critical fourth scene Theodora appears and says what she will do in the spirit-land for Strader, unless we have a feeling—though somewhat undefined, as is right at this point—that leads us to expect something. We shall not have the right feeling about what Benedictus means when he speaks in the same scene of an influencing of his vision, if we do not feel how into this vision come the forces of Strader's approaching death. To get the right feeling in the simple but very important eleventh scene, when Benedictus and Strader speak together, we must be aware of a premonition that something indefinite is approaching; and we best come to that by contemplating the connection between Strader's pictorial vision, together with his presentiment that the means he is using for the strengthening of his soul at times turns and injures his own soul,—and the words of Benedictus speaking of an influencing of his vision. The feeling of the approaching death of Strader is poured out over the whole development also of the other persons in this play, from the third scene onwards. If we combine this with what has been said concerning Ahriman as the Lord of Death, we shall penetrate more and more deeply into the knowledge that enters into the Mysteries of the Spirit, especially if we take into account how Ahriman plays into the mood of the drama which is influenced by the death-impulse of Strader.

Again, the last meeting, the significant meeting between Benedictus and Strader towards the end, and the last words of Benedictus spoken as a monologue, can only be correctly understood when we rightly comprehend the lawful and the unlawful interference of Ahriman in the world of the soul, and in the Word of the cosmic realms. These things are really not meant just to pass over the soul, we should continually enter more and more deeply into them. Not in order to criticise, but only to state an objective fact, it may be said that there are many signs, showing that the printed matter and courses of lectures which have appeared during the last three or four years have not been read in the way they should be, so as to arrive at all that has been implied and said, more or less obviously. That is not meant as a reproof. I am far from giving such; it is said because, to a certain extent, through all that is connected therewith, almost yearly at the close of our Course here at Munich such thoughts come to one's mind; thoughts which may remind us of the way in which our whole Anthroposophical Movement is placed within the present. We must consider the correct placing of this Movement in the present, in this chaotic life of the so-called present-day civilisation. We shall only be able to develop clear, watchful thoughts concerning the position of this Anthroposophical Movement if we bear one thing in mind above all. That is, that our civilisation will most certainly stagnate and dry up if it does not acquire the refreshment which comes from the sources of serious and genuine occultism. But, on the other hand, perhaps just such a course of lectures as this, which has perchance made us recognise the absolute necessity for turning to Anthroposophy or Spiritual Science, will lay something else on our hearts—it can lay something on the soul of each one of us. This may be described as the feeling of responsibility.

Very much of what is connected with the feeling of this responsibility and with the vision of the manner in which this movement of ours (necessary and non-deferable as it is) reveals also its faults and shadowy side—very much of this impresses itself deeply in the substrata of the soul. There one experiences much in regard to what kind of Movement ours ought to be, and what it only can be. This, though we can understand it, can really hardly be spoken in words, and he who fully feels it in his soul will prefer not to express it in words. For when it is realised, this responsibility frequently weighs souls down, and, thus realised, it first appears in a light that is quite deplorable, for on so many sides we see the many varied forms of Occultism appear to-day and side by side with them so little feeling of responsibility. For if, in truth, for the welfare of the evolutionary course of humanity and as the greatest and most beautiful thing that could come to pass in the present and the near future, we wish to see the growth of Anthroposophical wisdom, so, on the other hand we should like to welcome as the most delightful, the most beautiful, and oft-times the most satisfying thing that we should gladly see—the awakening of the feeling of responsibility in each of the souls influenced by our Spiritual Science. This appearing of the feeling of responsibility might indeed be valued even more highly.

We should consider this Movement of ours specially fortunate if, as it expands, we could see everywhere, as a beautiful echo, this feeling of responsibility. Many a one who himself thus feels it, would in a way be able to bear it more easily if he could more frequently perceive such an echo in the feeling of responsibility. And yet there are many things, future hopes, future expectations, with regard to which we must live in the faith and trust that the human soul, through its own intrinsic worth, will grasp the right and the true ; and that what must happen will really happen. As we separate after this course of lectures, we can clearly feel this ; for we would fain place firmly in each soul something that might awake and shine as enthusiasm for our Movement, but at the same time as a feeling of responsibility with regard to it. It would be the finest seal we could affix to our spiritual strivings, if we could all feel how, while in space we are no longer near one another, yet we are linked together by one of the most beautiful of bonds, that is, a genuine, true, spiritual bond, inspiring all souls with a similar warmth and enthusiasm for our Movement— a similar love for, and devotion to it, and at the same time with a feeling of responsibility for it.

And now as my farewell greeting to your souls, for the period in which we again separate after having been together for a time in space, may I give you this time the following parting wish : May the Truth of the spiritual life be strengthened ever more and more in our own souls and reveal itself, in that when we are not together in space we are still together, together through the fact that in us there lives the genuine enthusiasm which can light up our souls from an open-hearted and loving experience of our truth, together with a genuine, honest feeling of responsibility for what is to us so sacred and so necessary for the world. If we feel thus we shall be always together in the Spirit. Whether guided by our karma we be together in space, or whether our karma scatters us spatially for a while to our various occupations in life, we are still certainly together if we are joined by our enthusiasm and our feeling of responsibility. If we are, then we may have all hope, trust and confidence in the future of our Movement ; for it will then enter into our civilisation, into the spiritual development of humanity, even as it ought to do ; it will so find a home in it that we may perceive our Anthroposophy as a whisper out of the spiritual world, bringing warmth into our hearts. What ought to happen will happen ; and it must happen. Let us endeavour through this spiritual community of ours to become so capable ourselves that, so far as in us lies, what ought to happen, what must happen, shall happen through us.

CPSIA information can be obtained
at www.ICGtesting.com
Printed in the USA
BVHW010159240920
589464BV00009B/692